£19.75

Staffing Higher Education

Meeting New Challenges

also published for the OECD

Dimensions of Evaluation in Higher Education
Report of the IMHE Study Group on Evaluation in Higher Education
Urban Dahllöff, John Harris, Michael Shattock, André Staropoli
and Roeland in't Veld
ISBN 1 85302 526 7
Higher Education Policy Series 13

Evaluating Higher Education
Edited by Maurice Kogan
ISBN 1 85302 510 1
Higher Education Policy Series 6

Information Technology
Issues for Higher Education Management
G.M. Bull, C. Dallinga-Hunter, Y. Epelboin, E. Frackmann
and D. Jennings
ISBN 1 854302 542 9
Higher Education Policy Series 26

Higher Education Policy Series 27

Staffing Higher Education
Meeting New Challenges

Report of the IMHE Project on Policies for Academic Staffing in Higher Education

Maurice Kogan, Ingrid Moses and Elaine El-Khawas

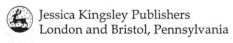
Jessica Kingsley Publishers
London and Bristol, Pennsylvania

OECD
OCDE OECD
PARIS

Project Team

Hans Acherman, Deputy Secretary-General, University of Amsterdam, the Netherlands

Elaine El-Khawas, Vice President for Policy Analysis and Research, American Council on Education, USA

Maurice Kogan, Director, Centre for the Evaluation of Public Policy and Practice, Brunel University, England

Ingrid Moses, Deputy Vice-Chancellor, University of Canberra, Australia

---

First published in the United Kingdom in 1994 by
Jessica Kingsley Publishers Ltd
116 Pentonville Road
London N1 9JB, England
and
1900 Frost Road, Suite 101
Bristol, PA 19007, U S A

for the OECD

© Organisation for Economic Co-operation and Development, 1994

Library of Congress Cataloging in Publication Data

A CIP catalogue record for this book is available
from the Library of Congress

British Library Cataloguing in Publication Data
Kogan, Maurice
Staffing Higher Education. – (Higher
Education Policy Series, ISSN 0954-3716;
No.26)
I.Title II. Series
378.1

ISBN 1-85302-541-0

Printed and Bound in Great Britain by
Bookcraft Ltd., Avon

Contents

Executive Summary

The following is a summary of the main issues covered and conclusions reached in this book.

Chapter 1 (Staffing as a Policy Issue)

1. Both the quantitative or demographic and the qualitative aspects of academic staffing policy and practice have been unduly neglected and need attention by policy makers at both the systems and the institutional levels, and by senior practitioners. Continued neglect will make higher education less capable of facing the challenges it must meet.

Chapter 2 (The Changing Framework for the Academic Profession)

2. The work of academics has become radically affected by several contextual factors: expansion and the movement from elite to mass and universal higher education; changes in expectations held of higher education; changes in its governance and the growth of quality assurance systems. These have affected the definition of higher education and the nature and status of the academic profession.

3. Higher education is experiencing changes in governance. Four main models of governance coexist with each other: the collegial, management, market and social utility models. Whilst it is inevitable that the managerial and market modes of operation will become stronger, it is essential to preserve the positive features of the collegial model.

4. A closer relationship between higher education funding and the economic health of the nation is expected. Curricula must become more directly relevant, subject to stake-holder

inputs and suited to the needs of employment. Faculty must now work with students, employer groups, the professions and government in ways not expected earlier.

5. There is a changing boundary with the non-higher education sector and this affects academic structures, with new hierarchies of institutions emerging. All of these changes, largely driven by policies of access, make it urgent to define higher education's mandate and boundaries.

6. Even when the need for more efficiency is taken on board, more staff will be needed to meet the new demands.

7. The professoriate have been 'proletarianised' and more than one single academic profession has emerged. The conditions and status of many staff groups have deteriorated.

8. Statuses of academics differ between countries and between institutions. Yet academics from different countries share much in common in terms of the academic content of their work.

9. Major changes have taken place in evaluation and accountability, from informal peer review to quality control mechanisms and from *ex post* to *ex ante* forms of assessment. These represent a shift from professional autonomy towards public accountability and have undermined the morale of individual academics. The quality and impact of quality systems need to be carefully monitored.

Chapter 3 (The Academic Profession: Changes in Task)

10. There are changing balances and tensions between different tasks: teaching, scholarship, research, consultancy, community service and administration. Priorities have to be made between them, by academics and institutions. Differentiation of task is taking place between institutions and within them.

11. Increasingly academics work within competitive and fluid environments along with greater uncertainty in institutional expectations. Ways in which multiple functions can be most fruitfully performed, both in the short term and over a larger period, need to be considered.

12. A new academic mandate is required. This will sustain the belief in traditional academic values – the disinterested search for the truth, and respect for logic, evidence and demonstrability – whilst supporting the dissemination and application of scholarly values to the needs of students and the wider society and economy. It requires that all higher education teachers are committed to publicly observable forms of disciplined enquiry.

13. The definition of research has expanded to include other forms of 'disciplined enquiry'. But whilst institutional mergers and the end of the binary line may offer more research opportunities to more individual academics, teaching and research are becoming increasingly divorced. The case for combining teaching and research remains strong. At the same time, the high priority traditionally given to research should be shifted in favour of greater recognition for teaching.

14. New forms of teaching and learning allow for stronger connection between knowledge acquisition and practice, and consideration of the needs of employment. Increased flexibility in teaching might result from the use of information technology and loosening up regulations of fixed teaching loads.

15. Responses to the market, including consultancy, bring opportunities but also diversion from core academic activity. The range of tasks involved in extra-mural, out-reach and continuing education add to the proliferation of academic work. Whilst they are an essential extension of the academic task, status problems may be experienced and call for greater institutional attention. The need for academic leadership is clear, but the danger of managerialism needs to be guarded against.

16. Changing forms of research sponsorship could lead to both wider opportunities and connections with practice, but also to 'epistemic drift'. In some countries research selectivity is reinforcing tendencies towards institutional differentiation.

17. In general, the widening of task and mandate requires both individuals and institutions to make priority choices. Also it

makes the case for systematic staff development based upon careful task analysis of individuals and their departments.

Chapter 4 (The Academic Profession: Staffing Structures in Response to New Demands)

18. Changes in task have brought with them changes in academic structures and appointments. The traditional formats remain strong but are not carrying the weight of changed circumstances. Different and often incompatible structures have emerged.

19. Part-time appointments, temporary full-time appointments and full-time appointments restricted to either research or teaching have enabled the system to carry its burdens. But the opportunities of non-tenured staff to move into permanent positions have deteriorated. They constitute a growing academic underclass who require system and institutional attention. There should be more systematic thought about the relationship between them and the full-time academic core staff. The presence of these two disparate groups do not meet present academic staffing needs and will pose serious problems over the long term. The reserve pool of junior staff is likely to be too small and not well-enough prepared.

20. Greater reliance is being placed upon the top-level academics to produce more high-quality research, to manage large research units, to carry a greater burden of curriculum design and external reporting and to develop and market new academic programmes. Tensions have grown, because of widening differentials in status and rewards, resulting in part from the widening of task.

Chapter 5 (Policies and Practices: Qualifications and Staff Development)

21. Although entry points and qualifications vary between countries, sectors and subjects, there is a continuing pressure of 'credentialism', but also doubt about the need for doctorates for all teachers.

22. Praxis experience has gained in importance but must be subjected to processes of disciplined enquiry and reflection.

23. Women and some ethnic groups continue to have different degrees of access to higher education posts and this needs greater attention and new strategies.

24. The changing range of tasks is shaping academic work patterns and qualifications. New career structures need to be considered. The Australian new career structure for its unified system might be a useful approach.

25. Selection for the academic profession is often based upon semi-tacit expectations which in some countries seem inappropriate to meet the changing range of academic work.

26. Preparation for the academic profession varies according to the point of entry, discipline and institution but especially for teaching is often unsatisfactory.

27. Preparation for the teaching function does not take account of the professional responsibility to develop, teach and assess in the subject areas. Teaching in higher education is largely without agreed standards, body of knowledge and skill, or peer review.

28. To assist academics with changing tasks and demands, including work with wider ranges of students, the changing research funding environment and preparation for leadership or administrative positions, more systematic and thoughtful use of staff development plans is needed.

Chapter 6 (Policies and Practices: The External Context. Staffing and Demography)

29. Governments and university leaders should grasp the importance of external trends affecting staffing needs for higher education. Demographic and economic changes add a critical dimension to the demand for higher education and faculty availability to meet it.

30. Traditional models of faculty demography assume a monolithic academic staff entering the profession and devoting entire working lives to it. A new generation of analysis describes a differentiated academic work force and takes account of economic factors and competing markets.

31. The core element of supply–demand models has been patterns of ageing among the academic workforce. These need to be complemented by studies of specific policy issues such as special concerns among disciplines, entrances to and exits from the profession at non-traditional times.

32. International flows and cooperation are increasingly relevant to staffing policy. International exchange must be monitored and encouraged but there are high costs to be considered at a time when resources are tight and many priorities are competing.

33. The staffing of Central and Eastern European institutions presents a separate set of issues. Problems of salaries, equipment and accommodation, and inability to recruit young researchers, are evident.

34. Graduate education is a key element in staffing for higher education but for the most part lacks explicit links to staffing policies. In many disciplines the universities have an uncompetitive position in the labour market. The uncertainties of academic employment affect the supply of able graduates.

35. The content of graduate education is being considered in some countries. Governments and institutions need to assess both the quantitative flows to graduate education and the kind of preparation offered within it, including whether the doctorate remains an essential prerequisite for higher education teaching.

36. Faculty should be regarded as a national resource. Institutions should be thought of as knowledge and skill banks within which a core staff will sustain continuity and leadership in research and teaching. They will attract able people who will take up subsequent careers in the many other occupations depending on disciplined enquiry. The system could then think more expansively about recruiting junior staff than happens at times when there are few vacancies.

Chapter 7 (Policies and Practices: Conditions of Service)

37. Policies affecting academic staff – including tenure and length of appointment, salaries and other rewards – need to be modified to allow for changes in role of established members of staff and to reduce gaps in status between tenured and non-tenured staff.

38. The dissatisfaction, reported widely and in many countries, of academic staff not only with remuneration and conditions of work but also with their roles, is a matter requiring attention by national authorities.

39. Remuneration is an important factor in satisfaction but as important are sufficient time for academic work and the general regard in which academic work is held. Current policy pressure, for evaluation, quality assurance and productivity gains, has added substantially to distraction and dissatisfaction.

40. Whilst the recruitment of women to higher education has improved in many countries, they still achieve a lower proportion of academic, and particularly senior, posts. To some extent this is the result of the lower recruitment to undergraduate courses in previous generations, but is still a matter requiring attention.

Chapter 8 (Policy Conclusions)

41. Governments should shed unnecessary regulation of academic work. It should be for institutions and the colleague groups in academic departments to decide on recruitment needs and how professional time should be spent.

42. National authorities should create a comprehensive needs analysis for academic staffing, based on estimates of needs for different types of staff in the light of likely demands for teaching, research and other higher education activities and a widening set of objectives. It should include micro-analyses of the precise nature of the academic task in different disciplines and institutions.

43. In anticipating staff shortages and surpluses more systematic thought should be applied to the use, on satisfactory and longer term contracts, of temporary and/or part-time academics.

44. Inter-institutional decisions are needed on the content of training for initial qualification and subsequent staff development. These should be differentiated to meet the changing and widening needs of students and of the larger range of tasks to be undertaken by faculty.

45. Universities should devise explicit staffing policies. Their establishment plans should be therefore linked to the whole institutional plans. Modelling of different academic work patterns would enable academic leaders to clarify the optimum conditions in which good work might be achieved. Elements of the analysis are suggested.

46. Academics as well as administrators should face the agenda of staffing issues as a professional as well as a managerial task.

47. Senior academics should analyse the conditions necessary to ensure that individual colleagues can meet their personal and collective objectives. Staff development programmes need to be taken seriously, and this entails academics working collaboratively with a properly resourced and professional staff development group.

48. There are gaps in both policy and practice, and in knowledge of higher education staffing. Not all countries have acquired a competent empirical and analytic capacity and governments are poor users of what knowledge already exists.

Chapter 1

Staffing as a Policy Issue

Academic staff are higher education's most important asset. More than anything else, it is the quality and numbers of its teachers and researchers which affects the ability of a university to teach its students and create and disseminate new knowledge.

Yet the staffing of higher education is a subject which policy makers at both the system and the institutional level have largely ignored. In this book we explore two kinds of issue. First, there is the demographic problem, which put simply is: how far will institutions be able to replace staff with those of the right quality in the years ahead, when so many of those recruited in the years of expansion will be leaving the system? Secondly, there are the qualitative issues: what kind of staff will be needed? How should they be recruited, prepared and developed and what conditions of service need to be provided? Neglect of these issues will affect the capacity of higher education to meet the new challenges being presented to it.

Demography and labour markets are part of the essential frame within which staffing should be considered. But so far not much has been written about the qualitative dimensions of faculty resources. The mandate for higher education has broadened and changed greatly over the last few years as a result of expansion, economic duress, the presentations of new demands by new types of clients, and changes in the map of knowledge. As the mandate moves more deliberately away from the pursuit of traditional academic goals, the formation and credentials of staff come into focus as a key issue. As the mandate changes, so do the institutional forms and structures of higher education, and it is within these that faculty will find new opportunities and restrictions. These changes are affecting too the vitality of institutions and the ways in which they work as a whole. The impacts of changes in function and clientele on forms of research and teaching and the resulting professional and managerial structures are among the subjects which we evaluate here.

The purpose and range of our project

In view of the evident importance of these issues the Directing Group of the Programme on Institutional Management in Higher Education (IMHE) of the OECD decided to mount a project that would bring together existing knowledge and attempt a policy analysis of the major issues. The project effectively began with a workshop for IMHE members in Paris in May 1992. Many of the papers produced then have appeared in *Higher Education Management* Vol 5 Issues 2 and 3, 1993. This report depends substantially on those contributions, all of which will be found listed as references at the end of this report. A project team was then convened and they have produced this report which in its turn will be the basis of workshops and conferences in 1994 and 1995.

In working on these issues, we set ourselves certain limitations. First, we could not undertake fresh research ourselves, but instead decided that we should bring together, in what is in effect a policy analysis, the results of work mainly of other principal scholars in the field. That now constitutes a considerable corpus of data and analysis, albeit largely based on the experiences of the English and French speaking countries, as will be seen from the list of references appended to this report. Indeed, a main concern should be that this often excellent work should be heeded by those responsible for higher education policy and management in OECD countries, and that other systems, too, will join the search for knowledge and analysis in this policy area. Secondly, we restricted ourselves to a study of academic staffing, whilst taking note, in Chapter 4, of the taking over of hitherto academic tasks by non-academic staff, and vice versa. Thirdly, we were not able to include any substantial consideration of the problems of staffing in Central and Eastern Europe, but have made some brief reference only (in Chapter 6) to faculty interchange and migration. Although the literature on these problems is sparse, these would certainly constitute a worthwhile agenda for study. And, of course, the staffing stocks of all parts of Europe, Australasia and North America will begin to affect each other as more migration, it is to be hoped in both directions, takes place. It is an intended part of our project development to work with colleagues in Central and Eastern Europe to establish some understanding of problems particular to countries outside the original arena of the OECD.

In offering this study, we are confident that it is both timely and that it addresses key issues. Systems and institutions are changing greatly in terms of both purpose and scale. Many will be recruiting large numbers of staff in the next decade. Whilst, as the key studies show, many of the planning boundaries will remain uncertain, policies and practices can at least be informed by knowledge of those uncertainties and the possible solutions that might be sought for them.

Chapter 2

The Changing Framework for the Academic Profession

In order to gauge the desirable sizes and characteristics of the academic calling, it is best first to examine the factors, changing radically as they have in recent years, that help shape its characteristics. In this chapter, therefore, we note the effects of expansion, of the changing expectations held of higher education by different stakeholders, of changes in governance, and of the introduction of public assurance systems. From this examination of contexts we go on to consider the impacts of these changes in terms of the changing definition of higher education, the extent to which higher education is staffed by a single or multiple profession and the changes in its status.

Movement from elite to mass and universal higher education

Academic staff work within systems that have undergone great changes. Perhaps the most important is the phenomenon of 'massification', a neologism denoting the shift from elite to nearly universal access in many countries. Trow (1974) generally regarded systems with a participation rate of below 15 per cent as elite. Beyond 15 per cent they move towards mass higher education and beyond 50 per cent towards universal higher education. Disregarding when the transition between these ideal types occurs in particular countries, and disregarding the particular percentages – some would maintain that qualitative changes occur well before the 15 per cent level is reached – it is clear that expanding student numbers changes the organisation, functions and nature of the student body and the academic staff. Indeed, 'higher education' itself changes. Whereas it once meant university education, it has come to include some education provided in a non-university sector, and, in the United States, forms of post-secondary education, e.g. in two-year community colleges, which do not lead to the award of first degree.

But many significant national differences persist, and within national systems faculty roles, status, salaries, working conditions and value-orientations vary between sectors. There are significant differences between the English-speaking countries and others. Almost all systems have been through the same evolutionary process. The German professoriate had been an elite group, belonging firmly to the upper middle class and preserved its privileges and status until quite recently. The system may have retained its traditional forms the longest, but eventually changed as drastically as any other.

The academic professionals now number many thousands of members in most countries – 600,000 in the USA with the largest system and the most inclusive definition of the academic profession, and more than 160,000 in Japan – and this loss of exclusivity has surely affected status. In the recent past, student numbers have determined the numbers of academics appointed to teach them, even when, as with UK university staff, time for research was implicated in their conditions of service; a provision now radically changed, for both teaching and research funds must be competed for *ad hoc*. The teaching–research nexus for the German professoriate, too, was well established. However, with the enormous expansion of student numbers and the government's attempt to utilise fully the capacities in the system, teaching demands have become the prerequisite for appointments and all staff are required to teach a minimum number of hours (Mommsen 1987). Over the past decades, growth in student numbers was not funded adequately and staff–student ratios deteriorated. Without new positions available, faculty were locked into their institutions with low chances of mobility. This increased faculty's perception of deterioration of working conditions. As we will note later in this chapter, these changes in scale have caused the expectations and content of higher education to become diversified.

Changes in overall structure

At the same time, partly as a result of increased size, but also because of a widening of purposes, there have been large-scale changes in structure although higher education systems in different countries have not enjoyed uniform natural histories. In many countries, hitherto separate parts, such as teacher training, have become part of university or near-university institutions, and unitary structures have emerged. In Finland, the Netherlands and Norway policy has been to create a parallel polytechnic sector with clear differentiation from the universities; France and Germany, too, retain differentiated structures.

There then has been an opposite tendency for binary systems to evolve into unitary structures, because the division is seen to become increasingly artificial, as the non-university institutions have become fully established. In Australia, institutional differentiation by function was successful only for a limited time and institutions from either side of the binary divide have been merged so that differentiation will be within institutions. In the UK all polytechnics were made universities and mergers were rare. In both systems, since functional differentiation cannot be avoided, new relationships and hierarchies of esteem within unitary systems are being negotiated. Where, as in Australia, the binary line is demolished by amalgamating universities with non-university institutions, negotiations and conflicts occur earlier and more visibly within the institutions themselves (Moses 1993b). In the UK, the reshuffling of statuses will take place with less apparent conflict because real differences of function will be obscured by the appropriation by the newly arrived universities of all of the academic plumage of the old. Differentiation there is likely to continue to be between institutions, although some shuffling of the hierarchy, and differentiation between institutions which previously belonged to the same sector, will gather pace.

Changing expectations of society

In the move from elite to mass to universal higher education, the functions which society and staff themselves expected universities to perform have changed. In elite systems the social, political and economic elite is largely recruited from the higher socio-economic strata and prepared for leadership positions by university staff, themselves in a privileged position. In mass higher education, elites are still being educated, but for a broader spectrum of professions and positions, with more emphasis on the transmission of skills (Trow 1974). With universal access the functions change to preparing the majority of an age group for a diversity of vocational roles in a post-industrial society. Access to higher education becomes a right, not a privilege.

Not all members of society can exercise this right equally – women and members of minority groups, in particular ethnic ones, are under-represented in higher education in general or in particular fields or level of study. Government initiatives may have attempted to redress this imbalance, notably in the USA, Australia and some Scandinavian countries where special admission rules, support systems and scholarships aim to address the imbalance in tertiary participation. In many countries access to higher education has become more equal between genders but the upper reaches of academic appointments remain largely male.

While access to higher education is seen as a civic right, there is also expected to be a direct relationship between funds spent on higher education and the economic health of the nation. Although no such relationship has yet been established there remains a powerful belief in the value of tertiary education as a national economic investment.

This is accompanied by an expectation that curricula will become directly relevant and that 'stakeholders' have legitimate input into type and content of courses offered. Similarly, universities are expected to share their expertise with society and members of the academic profession are urged to act as consultants, to work with professional organisations and collaborate with industry and other employers or clients for research.

The establishment and expansion of the non-university sector were fuelled by the desire to link higher education more directly to economic and social needs. Two decades ago Cerych and Sabatier (1984) noted that 'relevance' was problematic. Social institutions lag behind in their acceptance of the diversity of function and performance demanded by changing social needs, and employers, including government departments in some countries, despite rhetoric to the contrary, give preference to graduates from old universities, which retain their power to recruit the academically best qualified students. Thus the quest for relevance which may be aimed for more directly in institutions on the lower ranks of the status ladder leads to lower academic status, with abstract and non-utilitarian education more highly valued. Faculty with the highest claims to academic esteem, through their commitment to fundamental and theoretical research, remain the most protected. But they do so against a background of increasing lay control over higher education, and more pressing demands from wider client groups.

It is in responding to client needs and wants that higher education faculty might begin to perceive the greatest changes in their role and status. Their lack of responsiveness has almost certainly been exaggerated, as the enormous growth in occupation-specific masters' courses in the USA, UK and Australia demonstrates; differing degrees of responsiveness, across the subject range, have been observed, too, in undergraduate courses in England (Boys *et al*. 1988). Curricula have different structural characteristics affecting their permeability. Responses vary according to the degree of specificity related to jobs expected in particular employments (Silver and Brennan 1988).

Who are the clients of higher education? Faculty must work not only with students, both enrolled and prospective ones, but also employer groups, the professions and government. Governments have come to see higher education more than ever as an aid to the achievement of social and economic goals and increasingly expect it to be responsive to their agendas.

Changing student expectations

Over the past decades dramatic shifts in the student body have taken place. Young, male school leavers from high socio-economic background who were the main clientele of the universities in the period (and institutions) of elite higher education have been joined by an increasing number of young women, many of whom previously would have found places in separate but less prestigious institutions such as teacher training colleges, by men and women of all age groups, by part-time students in full or part employment, of members of socially and economically disadvantaged groups and of members of ethnic minorities. All of these groups expect that their educational aspirations will be met, although thus far most studies (in, for example, the Netherlands, Sweden and UK) show that there enrolment differentials persist according to socio-economic class.

Part-time students are on the increase and in some countries adults are the majority of the student body. The 'new clientele' includes both adults making a late start, and qualified personnel seeking continuing or work-related education. The two groups have different needs from each other and perhaps from those recruited straight from school and require different teaching strategies (Åhgren-Lange and Kogan 1992).

Students in a market economy, and particularly in those countries where they pay for higher education, are increasingly seen and see themselves as clients, even customers. Teaching is in many countries regularly evaluated and students expect academic staff to take notice of suggestions made. However, because of the transitory nature of student-status, voiced discontent often dissipates and commonly does not lead to action.

Students from other countries, particularly if they are fee paying students, have changed from beneficiaries of scholarship to becoming an economic force to be reckoned with and have increased their bargaining power accordingly. Education has become an industry and the educational market an international competitive arena. Students from Asia, in particular, exercise a customer's choice for courses in the UK, USA, continental Europe, Australia or Canada. They are thus equipped to be more critical and demanding, and this adds to the burdens of teachers who are not accustomed to customers' critique.

League tables, already familiar in the United States, are being published now in Canada and Britain, in Germany, the Netherlands and in Australia. Students are becoming informed on a variety of variables and can make more informed choices of course of study and institution than hitherto.

Expectations of employers

For some time employers have demanded that graduates not only have technical, professional or discipline-specific know-how but that they have generic and transferable skills. In the UK in the 1980s, initiatives were taken by government to persuade higher education institutions to address these assumed deficiencies. Values of industry and values of academe are not always compatible and the world of employment often is not able to present coherent, let alone uniform, demands for what it wants in its graduate labour force. In the Netherlands, for example, changes were introduced to the length of study in response to employers' complaints that students were too old on entering employment, and that they could learn skills on the job. Now the complaint is that they are too young and inexperienced.

Responsiveness seems to be most easily harnessed through incentive funding, e.g. for equity programmes, for industry–higher education collaboration, for introduction of work-related skills. In Britain, two schemes have made strenuous efforts to integrate into higher degree courses skills, experiences and values which are endorsed and promoted by employment. *Enterprise in Higher Education* is an incentive scheme with substantial funding from the British Department of Employment. Since 1988 the Initiative has offered competitive funding for projects submitted by universities which aim to develop students' generic skills, with an emphasis on experiential learning, resourcefulness and entrepreneurship (McNair 1990, Jones forthcoming). A second initiative, of the same time, is the Higher Education for Capability campaign, sponsored by The Royal Society for the encouragement of Arts, Manufacture and Commerce (RSA). It encourages the development of a range of skills and attitudes seen as desirable in graduates, among them: the ability to learn independently and collaborate with others, to set achievable and relevant goals, to acquire and apply knowledge and skills, to communicate ideas and information, to show respect and concern for others and to reflect on their values.

A different approach, though directed to the encouragement of similar skills, was adopted in Australia. A recent report by the Australian Business/Higher Education Round Table, *Educating for Excellence*, noted that business and higher education leaders sought graduates with high order communication skills, well-developed interpersonal skills, who were also numerate and economically literate, and, in view of Australia's current orientation, with an understanding of Asian culture and values. An analysis of Australian newspaper advertisements confirmed that a range of generic skills and attributes in graduates were sought by employers (Australian Higher Education Council 1992): oral and written communication as well as interpersonal skills, management and leadership skills, analytical, computer and research skills, skills in teamwork, supervision, organising and negotiation. Other more long standing schemes include US and Dutch polytechnic cooperative education, and British and Australian sandwich course arrangements, where work experience is matched to academic courses.

The implications of these developments are far reaching. They are a direct challenge to academics' monopoly of curriculum generation. They demand an extension of skills and a reorientation of teaching focus, as well as sharing of power with client groups.

Expectations of the professions

Professional bodies accredit university and college courses and can thus influence curricula and teaching. These bodies, too, have increasingly voiced concern about the standard of communication and interpersonal skills.

Many professional bodies demand a process of continuing professional education from their members. Some of these courses are delivered through higher education institutions, as non-award continuing education courses, as graduate diplomas or master's courses. For such courses academic staff must have both advanced subject matter knowledge and also knowledge of the professional context in which these students work and the applicability of what they teach to practice.

Changes in governance of higher education

Mass provision, economic duress, changing expectations, demands for more accountability have all contributed to the changes in governance of education that have taken place. They include changes towards managerial in place of collegial forms, towards market alongside academic criteria, and towards formulaic and quantitative in place of peer forms of evaluation. These have all made their mark on academic life and work and form part of the contexts within which faculty work.

Models of governance: the collegial

Four main models of higher education governance exist simultaneously, but with greatly different emphases in different times and in different systems (Becher and Kogan 1992, Birnbaum 1988). The traditional ideal has been collegial or professional. In this concept, groups of academics preserve the maximum of individual freedom to pursue the search for knowledge according to their own values and the demands of their disciplines. Collegial structures are minimal arrangements for ensuring that standards of entry are maintained and to enable distribution of resources among their members. The collegial model assumes that resources can be secured with a minimum of conditions either from endowments or from a benign state that assumes that what is good for academia is also good for society. Collegial values are most often realised in research universities where research and scholarship provide meaning to individuals, status and access to intra-institutional decision making. Leadership emerges from committee activities and autonomous academic activities (Bergquist 1992). Such a model has hardly ever existed in its pure state in terms either of relationships between government and institutions, or the internal governance of institutions.

The extent to which institutions are self-governing is an indicator of their status. Systems vary in the degree of central government control over the university as a whole, and this conditions the part played by the faculty. In many systems faculty exercise power over academic matters through senates, although in some countries lay members of bodies such as Council may also participate. In some systems a body formally superior to the senate – trustees or a council or governing board – is mainly concerned to exercise a financial or fiduciary role, and consists variably, according to country, either of a majority or wholly of lay non-academic members.

It should be noted that strong autonomy may simultaneously create collegiality among the most senior academics and a steep hierarchy (sometimes reinforced by national regulations) between the senior and junior members of the collegium. The distribution of power among different groups has changed considerably in most systems. In the late 1960s and the 1970s, the full professors lost some of their power to broader academic and student representation. But this trend was increasingly overlaid by the growth of central government and institutional authority over academic groups.

German universities are a clear example of the degree of change. A system of small autonomous units organised around a chair survived into the post-war period. Faculties controlled appointments, but curricular and examination standards were still the prerogative of chairholders (Mommsen 1987). However, following the reforms of the 1970s, *Fachbereiche* (departments) now organise the disciplines and in those *Länder* which implemented the reforms fully control the academic units. Chairholders lost many of their privileges, in particular automatic control of the research infrastructure associated with each chair. Associate professors were given the same corporate rights and middle-level non-professorial staff were given greater status and independence from the chairholder.

Democratisation led to *Drittelparität* – representation in the *Fachbereiche* was split equally between the professoriate, the non-professorial *Mittelbau* and students. The 'group university', that is, the university governed by group representatives, makes it more difficult to achieve academic self-government, because it incorporates non-academics alongside the academic staff. This will apply in most European countries where non-professorial academic staff succeeded in participating in a multi-partite government. Karpen (1993) notes this development particularly in France (mâitres de conference), Austria and Japan, while hierarchy is still best preserved in Switzerland.

Management model

The collegial model was most amenable to the conditions prevailing before massification and resource stringency. It now operates in parallel with the second model, that of management. In this the objectives of higher education are set by the state, the system or the institution, through varying degrees of negotiation with academia, and they form the frame within which academic discretion is exercised. State power may be exercised directly, as, for example, through the formal control maintained by some systems over the curriculum or over senior academic appointments. Increasingly, controls have been exercised indirectly through the assertion of outcome measures and *ex ante* forms of evaluation. The managerial culture values competence in managing people and finance, accountability and evaluation. Such cultures are more prevalent in institutions which concentrate on vocational education and training and service activities. Individual autonomy is more restricted and individual work more easily supervised. This managerial model is most often approximated in the non-university sector.

In Australia, 'managerialism' has been one of the features of the post-binary era, and similar trends were set in motion in the UK.

The Australian college and UK polytechnic sector were always more hierarchical with specific teaching and administrative functions attached to positions. Heads of School positions were largely managerial positions and the incumbents usually had a strong record of curriculum development and professional leadership, sometimes also in research. In the universities, there was adherence to a modified collegial model with most of the academic decision making occurring, or ratified, in committees.

In the 1980s, the decade of efficiency and effectiveness, the Australian government pushed strongly for managerial accountability. The newer universities, those evolving from the former college sector, first adopted the notion of accountability through line management. Some vice-chancellors called themselves Chief Executive Officer; deans and heads of departments were also in line management positions with specified accountabilities. Pro vice-chancellors were appointed in staff positions, accountable for quality and development of academic programs and research. The older universities followed suit, though the managerialism is tempered by the traditional collegial values. But devolution of budgets has meant for deans or heads of larger academic units line responsibility, and heads of departments increasingly are admonished to see themselves as managers.

Similar trends are observable in the UK, where the Jarratt Report (1985) also called for the reduction of the power of departments to set their own agendas and lent speed to the policy of outcomes measures. A normative literature on higher education management began to typify heads of departments as 'middle managers' (e.g. Lockwood and Davies 1985).

Market models

The third model is that of the market. In the use of this term, several modes of operation are often conflated. Higher education is increasingly involved in a 'real' market inasmuch as it offers priced services in competition with other institutions which may be other universities but equally may be private firms, as in, for example, consultancy work. Institutions also operate in the market for students, the labour market employing graduates and the market for faculty recruitment. The second kind of market is the competitive systems set up by funding bodies in which universities compete for funds and status. In the past academic reputation has been regarded as a kind of currency. Reputational currency, however, also attracts institutions' capacity to compete for real money. Now institutions compete for assessments of their competence which affect funding. Success in the market affects statuses inasmuch as it can determine positions on the academic ladder. It might be regarded as essential to institutional or subject survival and the approval of grant-making bodies and to decisions made by institutional managers. In both its priorities and mode of operation, however, it may prove inimical to the working of the collegial model.

The social utility model

The fourth model is that of social utility or welfare. This assumes that higher education enhances individual life chances and, as such, should be an important agent of policies for equality. A related assumption would be that higher education institutions should contribute to the life of their local communities and economies and in doing so lend strength to the growth of social cohesion. Such an approach advances such values as citizens' rights, equality, participation, and social usefulness. The social utility or welfare model would be the basis for policies and practice on access criteria and indeed on the nature of curricula and research agendas which might be in conflict with the professional and collegial model which tends to emphasise the specialist nature of the higher education task.

All models are relevant to the staffing of higher education. They affect missions and priorities and have an impact on the working lives of academic staff who have to locate their activities within the fields of force created by these models which are in tension with each other.

The collegial model went comfortably with the notion that decision making could be collective because all academics could undertake, more or less at their own volition, a mixture of teaching and research and share such other chores as administration. It was suited to a time when both resources and demands were conducive to non-directive forms of management. Assumptions of social utility were most prominent in the period of expansion in the 1960s. Market and management considerations have become more dominant over the last two decades.

Within, however, both the management and market models, decisions are shifted from the self-motivated individual, acting in circumstances of equal decision making, to managing a differentiation of tasks in response to external public policy or market pressures and reduced resources. Such decisions are likely to be taken by managers or through response to customer demands. The two non-collegial forms seem better suited to the performance of the wider range of tasks which demand that priorities are set, and the use of resources accounted for. But for good quality work to continue, higher education must ensure that the good features of the collegial model – self-initiative and a sense of intellectual freedom – are not lost as the other forms of governance take over.

Public quality assurance and its impact on individual and institutional autonomy

An important element of change in the governing patterns of higher education has been the growth of mechanisms for quality assurance. The most recent expansion of higher education came at a time of increasing financial stringency and, in many countries, a belief that state activity should be reduced. It is perhaps for these reasons that the accountability of institutions and the ways in which they spend public funds aroused new concern. With expansion, too, came sharpened interest in ways of maintaining academic standards.

In the past, universities largely determined their own standards by such methods as informal peer review, although key academic decisions, such as the appointment of professors, the award of research grants, and, in some countries, the award of degrees, were subject to somewhat more formalised external assessment. Non-university institutions in Australia and the UK were more restricted although increasingly free of external control as the ending of the binary line approached. Some courses have always been subject to external assessment by professional bodies; most obviously in medicine, engineering, education and social work.

The effect of new requirements is likely to be large, and represent a shift from the collegial model. The most drastic changes were made in the United Kingdom where those which were universities before the binary line disappeared in 1993 suddenly became subject to a range of public quality assurance measures. Research performance, from 1986, was assessed, the gradings published, and funding sharply differentiated between institutions. For teaching, the assessment machinery and vocabulary are even more complex.

Evaluation and quality assessment differ between countries. A national authority, as in the Netherlands and Sweden, might content itself with encouraging institutions to evaluate themselves and make use of their evaluations for internal developmental and corrective action, as a separate procedure from any evaluations the central authorities might make in allocating funds. In Australia, however, there is audit and assessment by a committee which recommends to the minister disbursement of additional funds.

Separate from the assessment of institutions is the question of modes of assessment. In the United Kingdom, quality assessment of research is summative and linked directly to allocations. It is not primarily intended for developmental purposes, except in an indirect and somewhat punitive way. Self-evaluation is not a predominant element of it, except inasmuch as institutions are required to set up their own quality control for teaching, which is itself subject to external audit. By contrast, in Finland, institutions are required to negotiate their mission with the Ministry of Education. This leads to a negotiation of targets in different areas. Institutions are expected to make their own self-evaluation in order to improve their own performance, and the self-evaluation does not form part of the allocative process. The Ministry, however, assesses the extent to which targets are met and adjusts the allocation of funds accordingly. Unlike in the UK, however, the adjustment can result in institutions in need of improvement getting more rather than less. In France, judgements made by the *Comité d'Evaluation* (Staropoli 1986) are stated to be for institutional self-development and intended to be formative rather than summative. But the evaluations are published in the press. In the Netherlands, too, it is claimed that the process is intended to be self-evaluative rather than external and summative.

A further important development of assessment systems in Europe is that they have moved from *ex post* to *ex ante* forms (Neave 1988). In *ex post* systems, broadly speaking, academics are trusted to determine their own objectives and ways of meeting them, and judgement, if any, occurs after the event. In *ex ante* evaluation, however, the system sets up objectives which have to be disaggregated and pursued within the institutions. They are then judged on the extent to which national objectives are met. In most cases, too, allocations are tied to the judgements on the extent to which objectives are met.

The impact of these changes is likely to be great. In the most rigorous systems, it is assumed that academics will perform better if their performance is evaluated and judgements made public. Evaluation is used to reward the 'best' and to reduce the funding available to the 'worst'. In fact, in the UK it is believed that many research centres and individuals of merit, if not of the highest excellence, have suffered both loss of funds and prestige and the model is therefore thought to be purgative rather than developmental (Kogan 1993). At the same time, with the increased differentiation and massification traditional modes of evaluation have obviously become insufficient. If summative and quantitative forms of evaluation can lead to injustice and callow judgement, so it can be argued that historic judgements about who and what are best also favour those already established and may give no place to new forms of learning.

Definition of higher education

These changes make the need to redefine higher education, and to restate its mandate and boundaries, all the more urgent.

Three dimensions are relevant here. The first concerns the extent to which there is a higher education essentialism, that is, whether it is bounded by certain assumptions and values. The issue has become sharper because higher education has expanded its functions in ways that take it further away from its original academic tasks. It seeks to make its usefulness more obvious to funders, and many institutions, but particularly the most vulnerable, will become more job-related in their offerings. At the outer boundaries at least higher education has admitted forms of knowledge transmission and enquiry that approximate more to training and consultancy than to higher education in its traditional and 'essential' forms. These considerations concern, therefore, what kind of knowledge is generated and transmitted by higher education.

We assume that higher education based research is to be distinguished from activities such as consultancy, the objectives of which are set by the funder rather than the consultant, and that scholarship is different from serious journalism. Education is distinguishable from vocational training by virtue of its mandate to criticise and to present forms of knowledge alternative to those that at present exist; only as a secondary function might it be concerned with the transmission and inculcation of established knowledge and techniques. Academics may engage in consultancy, journalism or training, but they are not higher education's core activities. These instead derive from the creation and use of knowledge that is tested, verified and applied according to the rules of logic, evidence and demonstrability which academics themselves create. Higher education teaching follows the same principles in its concern to enhance the ability to criticise and advance the existing stock of knowledge.

The second defining characteristic is the institutions in which higher education takes place. Here the definitional difficulty concerns the teaching rather than the research function. We take higher education to mean those forms of post-school study which take place in institutions staffed by those who are engaged in or conversant with the products of knowledge derived from research or scholarship. This thus includes those institutions in which all or most teachers are researchers yet also those whose teachers are more concerned with the application and transmission than with the generation of knowledge but whose work is grounded in current research, development and scholarship.

A third dimension is that of level. It is a hard task for comparativists to determine how far, for example, the institutions in the USA, which range from majestic research universities to community colleges providing two year courses, or of Japan that are similarly stratified but in all take 40–50 per cent of an age group, should be all defined into higher education status. They compare with such countries as, say, the Czech Republic or the UK, where until recently higher education has not extended beyond 12–15 per cent of the age group. In their turn such criteria determine the kind of faculty required to perform its functions and how they will be stratified according to the knowledge objectives.

In some countries US community colleges would be regarded as part of the further education sector. Yet in, for example, the UK, further education colleges have undergone a considerable change in status and are now incorporated bodies free of local authority control. The expansion and reordering of higher education may lead to a redefinition of boundaries with further education. Particular practices are already leading in this direction. Universities may franchise some teaching in non-university institutions. Regular arrangements are increasingly made for transfer of students at the end of one or two years of a further education course to a university.

The emergence of a multiple profession

These large framework changes are affecting the nature of academic work which is already complex, and uncertain of its definition and boundaries. Is there an academic profession and what does it mean to belong to it? Traditionally, higher education has been staffed by those who may claim professional standing as scholars, priests and ministers, scientists and teachers. Only relatively recently have we come to speak of an academic profession, or academic professions, and then mainly in the American (Finkelstein 1984, Clark 1987), British (Perkin 1969, Halsey 1992, Fulton 1993) and Australian literature (Moses 1992a).

In post-industrial societies higher education qualifications have become the entry requirement for most professions, including para-professions; hence higher education has become socially and economically a key institution and government, professional groups, industry and business all seek an active part in shaping it, in making it 'relevant'. Yet its own professionalism is uncertain and not universally homogenous.

If there is an academic profession, it is still quite different from others. Academics do not share a discipline base; their tasks are complex, loosely defined. There is little (though increasing) accountability, there is tension between the ambitious goals inherent in academic work and the success which faculty perceive they achieve (Teichler 1993). Perkin (1969) aptly named it the 'key' profession because it differs from the others by recreating itself and providing the training for the other professions.

If we define a professional as one who possesses esoteric knowledge shared only with others in the same profession, physicists, historians, sociologists and biochemists are not in the same profession. But although they remain part of their disciplinary grouping, while engaged in a university environment they share conditions, status and functions. A shared belief in such values as the need to demonstrate the evidence and logic behind statements, or an altruistic concern for one's students, might bond together otherwise disparate groups into one profession. At the same time, the range of interests, functions and statuses incorporated into higher education is now so wide that the concomity noted as existing across a wide range of institutions and statuses (Trow 1974) may be difficult to sustain. At the same time, as in many other sectors, a 'new professionalism' may be emerging which emphasises the qualities associated more with the managerial and market than with the collegial model: namely, the capacity to work in teams, to be cost conscious and results orientated, to respond to exogenous criteria of quality, and to be able to create and sustain networks both within and across the higher education boundary.

There remains the question of who is recognised as part of the academic profession. In the Anglo-Australian systems all academic staff employed in higher education institutions are members. As already noted, these include both universities and more vocationally oriented institutions such as colleges and polytechnics. Academic staff may be called 'professor' in institutions of all types and ranks, as in the United States. Elsewhere they may have a title which carefully designates both type of institution and rank within it. The use of the title is becoming more diffused in both Australia and the UK as more institutions and wider groups of staff, including non-academics, feel they can lay claim to full academic status.

In some countries, however, for example, Germany and France, academics would have difficulty with the concept that a full academic career necessarily involves both teaching and research (Clark 1987). French higher education, for example comprises three main sectors, the *grandes écoles*, the universities, and the research institutes. Each has a different history, and institutional organisation and culture as well as faculty career patterns (Friedberg and Musselin 1987).

Proletarisation

As we have already noted, most OECD countries have moved from elite higher education to mass higher education, with some countries well on the way to universal higher education. This shift has effected a status shift in the academic profession. Halsey (1992) speaks of 'proletarisation' in an analysis of the British academic profession. He attributes this to reduced power and advantage in its work and market position, security of employment, and chances of promotion. However, while from the perspective of university faculty this is true, other groups within the academic profession, notably those from the former British polytechnic and Australian college sectors, have advanced in status and chances of promotion, whilst also suffering worse working conditions because of the less favourable staffing ratios and funding. Mass higher education has led to a deterioration in working conditions in all countries. Apart from the changing conditions for permanent staff, there are also many groups of faculty in marginal non-tenured positions with little access to the resources, privileges and status academic work traditionally bestows. Their chances of permanent or long term contract work have deteriorated even further (see also Chapter 4).

It has been argued, however, that because higher education has become increasingly recognised as important to economic and social development this has increased 'the weight' of the academic profession. Nevertheless, the perception of most academics is that status and autonomy have been reduced alongside attempts to make higher education an instrument of the economy and more subject to 'steerage'. At the same time it is true that there are aspects of academic life that remain advantageous and some that have improved for some. The expansion in the number of academic staff occurred mostly in non-professorial and junior positions, and in many countries they were able to gain social security and tenure and participation in the corporative bodies. With the exception of Great Britain, in European countries professors are civil servants and on tenure; non-professorial academic staff in Great Britain and Australia enjoy tenure and social security to an extent which their continental colleagues in France, Italy and Austria have been aspiring to in the last few years.

Non-monolithic nature of the academic profession

The academic profession is, then, by no means undifferentiated. We will see in Chapter 4 that in each country there are differences between institution types and within institutions. In the statuses accorded, in numbers of staff and in proportions of senior to junior staff, systems differ greatly, and there are also wide differences within national systems. These facts make it all the more surprising that academics from different countries find so much in common with each other when working on the academic content of their research and scholarship. The international dimensions of knowledge and scholarship override the differences in material provision and legal and social statuses. Is this perhaps proof of a common culture or essentialism?

Implications

We have argued here that whilst higher education may be thought of as sustaining its own boundaries they have moved greatly as institutions shift from providing for the elite to providing education for a mass or universal clientele with a greatly increased range of expectations. Hitherto protected positions have become 'proletarianised' and the profession has become increasingly diverse and multiple. From the perspective of this study, several consequences follow from these changes:

- As a result of growing numbers, the amount of resource provided for each student is bound to go down as numbers increase. All the same, more faculty will have to be recruited to cope with more students and a wider range of tasks.

- As numbers increase so will the diversity of the clients, their expectations and the demands they make on higher education faculty.

- It follows that faculties will change their profile of qualifications and principal interests. As higher education moves more certainly into mass provision, the make-up of the teaching force is likely to change; the proportion of staff mainly interested in research will be reduced and the social and professional dynamics of the academic calling will change.

- Massification leads to the functional differentiation and reordering of the hierarchy of institutions and the statuses of the staff in them. This might be reinforced by government imposed selectivity in the allocation of funds for research and advanced teaching, but it will also result from the academic profession itself sorting out institutions and departments into ladders of esteem.

- Modes of government will change partly as a result of the same forces that have led to massification, and partly as a result of massification itself. Whilst it is inevitable that the managerial and market modes of operation will become stronger, in order to bring about clearer definition and differentiation of roles, it is essential to preserve the positive features of the collegial model.

- Decision making about quality issues, and decisions on resources that rely on judgements of quality, have shifted from institutions and academic groups within them to quality assurance mechanisms prescribed or administered by the larger system. This has affected the self-confidence of individual academics who might be distrustful of the nature of the judgements and the consequences of them.

- At the same time, the expansion of systems and the breakdown of traditional hierarchies of quality might necessitate more systematic quality assurance than has hitherto existed. If so, its quality and impact need to be carefully monitored.

- In the next chapter, we will note how the academic task in many countries is becoming wider. This will call upon a wider range of qualifications and training for faculty.

These changes largely add up to new constraints on academics. A changing mandate and a wider range of tasks may also open up new opportunities. It is to these that we now turn.

Chapter 3

The Academic Profession
Changes in Task

Changing balances and tensions between different tasks

With the growth of expectations, almost all institutions and their staff are under pressure to widen their range of tasks. In some countries, universities' functions remain traditional and linked almost wholly to research, scholarship and teaching. In other countries, they have broadened to a point where some academics must make priorities between them or even change their work profiles. A balance must now be struck between teaching, scholarship, research and administration, with consultancy and community functions occupying an increasingly prominent place in the life of some campuses. Whilst not all academics pursue all of these activities, many are expected to engage to a significant degree in many of them, to the point where they may feel distracted from the main traditional academic tasks.

Boyer (1990) pleads for a new conceptualisation of academic work in which all of its emanations are deemed scholarly activities but should be seen as four separate but overlapping functions: the scholarship of discovery, the scholarship of integration, the scholarship of application and the scholarship of teaching. Rice (1990) also defines academic work in all of its forms as scholarly work related to knowledge. He distinguishes between advancement of knowledge, integration of knowledge, application of knowledge and representation of knowledge. Lynton and Elman (1987) assert that 'professional activity is an *extension* of traditional scholarship, not a *substitute* for it'. Hence it needs to be rewarded, as it is in the polytechnic/college sector.

The new academic tasks

The changing environments of structure and expectations have caused staff roles and institutional expectations to become fluid and uncertain. Academic work now has dimensions which are beyond many individuals' abilities and, perhaps, inclinations, whilst at the same time creating new challenges and opportunities. Academics must gear their teaching to both bright school-leavers and ill-prepared ones and to mature, part-time, first-generation and non-native language speaking students. They must be aware of and avoid culture- and gender-specific language and examples, and use plain language – and simultaneously enthuse, stimulate, instruct, motivate, train and prepare students for life-long learning and immediate professional usefulness.

At the same time expectations of teaching standards might become more formalised yet staff get little help in assessing how to reconcile responsiveness to student and employer demands and one's own scholarly standards and discipline-wide standards.

Even in those institutions with no history of research, there has been 'academic drift' or a tendency for staff to attempt to build up their research programmes. It seems likely that as many non-university institutions are awarded university status, these attempts will increase, and with them a broadening of the definition of research. Faculty in 'new' universities may work hard to establish a full academic mandate for forms of disciplined enquiry which fall outside the traditional definitions of research. These would be systematic attempts to conceptualise problems from working life and develop good procedures for tackling them.

There will be, then, strong efforts to sustain the combined role of teacher and researcher. Even if government policies do not support research by all academic staff, most believe that they are expected to conduct research, and many want to. Faculty, in differing degrees, will therefore be expected to:

- devise projects which can be funded and will attract funding, which will have commercial use, which will sustain research students, will be suitable for group, interdisciplinary, or industry research
- be able to market their research to companies and the media, to write scholarly papers and for the press, to impress colleagues at conferences and the public through TV appearances

- attract research students and to maintain a balance between advising and directing so that students obtain their research degree in minimum time having completed an independent piece of research while receiving training

- be aware of occupational health and safety regulations, ethical clearance and practice, intellectual property and other regulations

- be part of the peer review process by refereeing manuscripts and grant proposals, promotion and selection applications, and examining honours, Master and PhD theses for their own and other institutions (Moses 1992a).

Lynton and Elman (1987) propose that every faculty member should be involved in both departmental and non-departmental teaching and professional activities. Every faculty member would continue to be firmly based in his or her discipline and would be evaluated in part for pertinent teaching and scholarly work. In addition, many faculty members would also participate in one or more multidisciplinary units and have their work evaluated by their peers in those groups. They argue that applied research and technical assistance, professional education, opportunities for interaction with the workplace and relationship with practitioners are both needed and provide those academic staff not at the cutting edge of basic research with new opportunities for stimulating and productive scholarship.

But if many more academics will receive a wider academic mandate, it seems obvious that not all academics can undertake all of these tasks. Given the drive towards research which carries higher status and professional rewards, decisions will have to be made about who does what. This trend towards differentiation will reinforce managerial rather than collegial ways of working. The proliferation of work may also justify the employment of a more varied and flexibly managed faculty group.

While there are exhortations to value various forms of scholarship and contributions to knowledge in a mass higher education system with a greater variety of institutional mission, the tensions between the various functions often are not acknowledged. It will be essential for institutions and departments to clarify the ways in which resources, particularly staff time, will be allocated between these tasks, and that individual members of staff are counselled on how to shoulder what may be more diversified patterns of work.

Teaching and research

In the traditional university, particularly those following the Humboldtian tradition, it was assumed that established faculty would be engaged in both teaching and research or scholarship. Two major exceptions to this assumption were the division of French higher education between the elite *grandes écoles*, wholly committed to teaching, and the universities where both teaching and research take place, and the Swedish division of function, started in the 1960s and now being abandoned, between *lektors*, wholly engaged in teaching, and *docents*, wholly engaged in research.

In many systems of higher education, however, teaching and research are organisationally divorced. Though universities may combine teaching and research, there are also teaching-only and research-only institutions. What organisational form makes teaching most effective, what research? Academic staff in a variety of countries when surveyed (USA, UK, Australia, Germany) (Boyer forthcoming) believed that teaching and research mutually benefit, stimulate and enrich each other and most are teaching-cum-research oriented – they prefer to do both, albeit with varying emphasis.

Yet some national policies are leading to separation of teaching and research, and that might abbreviate the new mandate. In existing universities with a tradition of research, research selectivity is causing some departments to analyse the activities of their individual members. In order to give time to the more productive researchers, those less capable of producing published work might be required to take the heaviest teaching and administrative burdens. Within a predominantly research environment some workloads could consist wholly of teaching and administration. Such a differentiation of tasks among members of academic departments has been discussed in the US, mainly as a way to increase the overall 'productivity' of departments.

Is teaching best combined with research? Is teaching better where it is the primary function? An Australian study (Moses and Ramsden 1991) found that college staff on the whole placed greater value on good teaching whilst university staff tended more to promote student independence. In another study, Australian academics supported both values of good teaching practice and student independence, more than did German academics (Moses 1993a). Various national discipline reviews found that students and graduates from the former college sector rated the teaching they received in their institutions higher than did university students or graduates. But there is no conclusive evidence that teaching in particular types of institutions is always more effective than in others.

The direct link between research and graduate teaching is often acknowledged. Much less is the role of research and publication in facilitating general student learning. Perkin (1987) stresses the importance of research and publications, for, among other things, student learning: 'Publication, it is often forgotten, is a vital form of teaching, as reading is a vital part of learning, and although the immediate connection between research and good teaching may be exaggerated, nonpublishers do not necessarily make better teachers. On the contrary, those who cannot explain themselves in print often cannot explain themselves in class.'

Productivity in research and related areas is influenced by the institution's emphasis on various functions and the opportunities for staff to conduct and get it funded. However, within one Australian research university, academic staff in the research institutes with no undergraduate teaching obligations did not have higher research productivity than those teaching at both undergraduate and graduate level. In Australia, there is a significant difference between publication rates of university and (former) college staff (Moses and Ramsden 1991). In the UK, no former polytechnic received as high a rating as an 'old' university in the 1993 research rating exercises. It remains true that if teaching loads are not heavy and research funds are available, teaching and research are compatible and lead to high productivity in research.

Throughout higher education, in fact, the onset of massification and of functional differentiation at both the institutional and individual academic level, whatever the structure of the total system, is raising issues about the relationship between and the priority accorded to different tasks. New and meaningful definitions are needed. 'Disciplined enquiry' can be taken to include development as well as research, including such activities as curriculum development and consultancy. Where does the spectrum contained within 'disciplined enquiry' begin and end? When does it become non-academic consultancy and development work? What forms of work merit which forms of academic recognition? Traditional criteria of objectivity, demonstrated logic and evidence remain firm. But are other criteria embedded in the needs of praxis and client groups legitimately to join them?

These issues will become more prominent in those systems which have reshaped themselves. In Australia, the college and university sectors were already beginning to converge in many of their characteristics (Moses 1991b). The Australian 'Unified National System' (UNS) created by a Labor Government has a strong egalitarian basis. Some of the values and functions of one sector were adopted by the other. Programmes, courses, service to students and outside groups, and consultancy, highly valued in the non-university sector, were increasingly so by the universities. Specialisation through research was difficult to achieve in the college sector, but many of their academics nevertheless strove to become part of the international disciplinary community and to participate in peer activities (Moses and Ramsden 1991). A significant number of staff achieved this against the odds. In fact, twenty years ago, Trow (1974) noted 'a genuinely egalitarian policy must allow every institution to attract people who are innovative intellectually, and that means supporting their research and giving them the high degree of autonomy they need to create new knowledge, new fields of study and new combinations of disciplines.' In other systems, too, client expectations and changes in structures will elicit similar shifts in orientation and questioning of mission.

New forms of teaching and learning

Not only the content but also the organisation of teaching is shifting from that of the autonomous individual teaching from a specialist knowledge base to more publicly controlled sequences administered through modular and other systems intended to produce flexibility and student choice.

In many universities, too, there are attempts to permeate the curriculum with the results of new approaches to the educational needs of students. These are underpinned by major shifts in theories of knowledge: from contemplative to action theories in which knowledge development and knowledge acquisition are seen as related to practice; and the shift from cognitive to holistic personal development. Both sets of ideas can be used to underpin the emphasis on skills in higher education but also point to the limitation of skills as organising principles of learning.

Such developments, which have been the subject of detailed study (e.g. Boys *et al.* 1988, de Weert 1992), have an impact on the traditional organisation of knowledge into disciplines. There is a discernible shift in undergraduate teaching towards forms of curriculum which allow for more multidisciplinary work and for student exercise of options. This move towards modular structures also affects academic organisation because it requires the creation of matrix structures which embody both discipline-based departments and cross departmental groupings of teachers and examiners. To teach in such settings may also require teachers to move from didactic towards experiential forms of learning as is being attempted in the UK Enterprise in Higher Education Initiative (Jones forthcoming). These moves, in their turn, raise questions about the training of future teachers in higher education which may not be satisfied simply by the acquisition of a research-based doctorate.

A related set of considerations concerns the extent to which curriculum is permeable by or responsive to the needs of employment. The outcome is to some extent subject-specific inasmuch as some courses have always been related to the perceived needs of particular occupations (Silver and Brennan 1988), although the majority (e.g. two-thirds in the UK) of graduates acquire employment in areas not related to their courses of undergraduate study. Even where, however, undergraduate instruction is not directly connected to particular job destinations, in some systems at least, there is concern to ensure that undergraduates have the opportunity to possess generic working skills, such as the capacity to work in teams, the ability to express clearly and to organise one's work, and the ability to use information technology. To these a UK government agency would add the objectives of learning 'effective use of resources to achieve targets, taking responsibility effectively, and an understanding of the business environment' (McNair, 1990).

Where they are occurring – and in many systems teaching remains formal and didactic – these changes represent important moves away from the traditional Humboldtian concept of the researcher – teacher inducting apprentice scholars into the mysteries of the academic task. They challenge the content and format of the curriculum, and the teaching skills of teachers who are to some extent invited to share the power to generate the curriculum with groups outside their own departments or faculty or even their own university. Academic staff will need to develop skills to work well with those outside who may have a great deal to contribute to the teaching and research activities of higher education.

Distance learning and information technology

As OECD countries approach mass higher education, alternatives to teacher-centred teaching have to be explored for economic reasons. Thus, in Australia, the government have sponsored large-scale projects investigating 'open learning', developing computer-based education and interactive multi-media packages, use of satellites, use of video conferencing and the like. Whilst it has not been established that the use of technology decreases education costs, there are some studies which demonstrate benefit to the student.

A recent study of computer-based education in Australia (Cochrane, Ellis and Johnston 1993) noted that it was most often used in mathematics/computing, sciences, health sciences, the broad area of business and law studies, engineering processes and humanities. Students found it useful for reinforcing material to be learned and preparation of assessments. Staff found that producing material took a lot of time but that though their own time use might not be reduced, fewer tutors were necessary to work with small groups of students.

If driven by an educational agenda, new forms of teaching stress cooperative and collaborative learning tasks which promote integration of professional or disciplinary know-how with generic skills and a commitment to independent and lifelong learning.

So, too, might information technology affect the social organisation of teaching and the role of the university teacher. The earlier uses were attempts to transfer knowledge from the teacher to the taught but 'they were expensive to produce, and deliver and there has been little leverage' (King 1990). Much more successful has been the use of powerful and general computer tools to fundamentally change the content, sequence, and mode of instruction. Tools such as word processing, spreadsheets, database systems and the like have been used to dramatically improve courses. 'In courses that use these tools, faculty have moved from presenters of information to participants in learning' (King 1990). If most teachers would not regard themselves as mere 'presenters of information', these new modes of data analysis and presentation, and the ability to model material which was hitherto the subject of didactic transfer, could have powerful effects on curriculum, at least in some subjects. They shift the balance of power from the expert in the subject to those who are capable of making most use of sophisticated systems. These changes again present challenges to staff preparation for the teaching role, although it is clear 'that whilst the impact of information technology on research is enormous ... in the instructional area there is no sign that the computer will replace the lecturer' (Arms 1992).

Increased pressures on teachers

Except in the most highly favoured institutions pressure is being exerted on academics to teach more students, both undergraduate and postgraduate. As we have seen, in many institutions, the teaching load is not only heavier but also more multiple, to meet the needs of wider groups of clients. Massification is not being funded by commensurate increases in staffing and the result is increased teaching loads. The pressure to take more students, at lower costs, and the competition for resources and status in research and scholarship, create hard choices for individual academics. At the same time, selectivity, quality assurance and other public policies generate a great deal of new administrative work.

Fixed teaching loads

The working requirements of teachers vary greatly in different countries and different levels of institutions. In some countries, teachers are required to complete a statutory number of teaching hours each year, and this is thought to produce rigidity in the way in which academics use their time and in the formats of the curriculum. Fixed hours may also encourage teachers to restrict their contacts with students. Attempts are being made in some countries to give discretion to universities in these matters (Konttinen and Välimaa 1990). But this may be occurring at the same time as universities in other systems, where such restrictions would be deemed contrary to the conditions of professional working, are beginning to calculate the amount of time spent on different tasks. Or this can happen within departments facing heavier loads in an attempt to secure equality of burden between staff members. Under economic pressure professional notions of working may regress to managerial forms of calculation.

Research

Changing patterns of prescription and sponsorship-based research

The research function of universities in almost all subject areas has grown massively in size and strength since 1945. For the most part higher-education-based research has been located within universities rather than non-university institutions, although in some systems (e.g. Finland, France, Germany and Norway) a major proportion of publicly funded research has been located in non-higher education institutes.

Inasmuch as research and scholarship has been assumed to be connected with the teaching function, their funding was included in substantial part in core grants which provided for university staff time and laboratories, workshops and equipment. Additional resources, some of them substantial, could be sought from research councils, and in some countries, particularly the UK and the USA, from private foundations. These arrangements were well suited to the assumptions that research should be moved primarily by academic curiosity and the disinterested search for knowledge. Funds for applied research and development were also sought from industrial or government sponsors, but these were regarded as second order activities, and sometimes with suspicion as coming from tainted sources.

Theoretical research is still most highly regarded, but the funding scene has changed radically over the last two decades and this is affecting research objectives. In some systems, e.g. the UK, core funding no longer guarantees staff time and other resources for research must be sought, ad hoc, in competition between research centres. Research councils remain an important source of independent funding, but they have increasingly moved themselves to be responsive to what they see as the demands and needs of government and industry and commerce (Becher, Henkel and Kogan 1993). In order to continue to play a part in the research world many academics feel compelled to seek contracts in applied work, some of which are for short periods of time and to be completed at short notice.

Governments have sought to establish new and closer connections with the setting of research objectives. In the UK the notion of 'strategic' research embodies the belief that there are forms of fundamental research which can be related to the solving of practical problems. Recently the UK government have announced the creation of a Forecast Unit (White Paper 1993) which will link the needs of users to the capacities of the researchers.

Anxieties have been voiced that these trends are likely to lead to 'epistemic drift' (Elzinga 1985). This concerns the extent to which not only the objectives but also the knowledge rules governing research would be bent by pressure from sponsors. It is certainly true that research agendas have increasingly responded to sponsors' demands, but whether that has affected research procedures and standards remains a subject for further empirical enquiry.

Changing location and funding of research

The ability of sponsors to put pressure on universities is reinforced by the reduction in core funding by government, and by the growth of research capacity outside universities. We have noted that in some systems government funded institutes might be primarily concerned with development rather than research; in some countries, however, they undertake research which would find a place in university departments elsewhere. Other competition is presented by the growth of research capacity in private sector firms, particularly in such social science areas as evaluation research where there is increasing competition from powerful private consultancies. To some extent academics have been compelled to move their sights and change their working practices. Previously, they might have been able to negotiate a fully funded project lasting two or three years or more whereas at present many subjects which they consider worthy of deeper exploration are funded in order to get quick answers.

In some countries, and the UK is again the leading example, universities which previously could rely on core funding as an unchallenged source of research funds are now required to compete in research selectivity exercises. Each cost centre is assessed every four years on a five grade scale, largely by a process of peer

review. The research gradings have a substantial impact on resource allocations; the grades are published and they further affect
the ability of different universities to attract research funds and
students. Such systems are part of an explicitly selective policy
intended to further differentiate institutions on a teaching–research spectrum.

A less tensile relationship exists between research and scholarship than between the two and consultancy. In principle, research
is the discovery of new knowledge whereas scholarship is the
reordering and reconceptualisation of existing knowledge. Advanced work in some parts of some disciplines, for example philosophy and the study of classical texts, may consist almost wholly
of scholarship. The usefulness of scholarship is perhaps under-
stated. There is so much new knowledge being created that critical
assessment and ordering of it would be helpful not only to teachers
but also to researchers. The recruitment of more diverse undergraduate clienteles also seems to demand the preparation of text-
books suited to their needs, but based on the latest research
findings.

Other tasks

Working in the market

Institutions in those countries where Welfare State assumptions
have given way to a market model are being impelled to enter the
priced market by encouraging their academics to engage in fee
producing consultancy and short courses directed to particular
users. This produces both opportunities and problems. Additional
resources reduce dependency on public funds and bring degrees
of freedom with them. Used properly they can fund some of the
fundamental academic activities that might otherwise go short of
resources. They enable individual academics to enhance otherwise
modest remuneration. At best they enable academics to sustain
contact with, and to test, theory in the world of practice.

The potential problems are that they may divert efforts from
core academic activities to work set according to the agendas of
those who pay for the consultancies. Care must therefore be taken
to ensure that the consultancy is compatible with the academic
style and objectives of the academic base. They may also cause
manifest inequity between those who work a full week at the

departmental base on an academic salary and those who may receive high fees whilst sustaining their academic privileges and facilities. There are also different consultancy opportunities for different disciplines, and it is not always the ablest minds in the hardest subject areas who receive the largest rewards. Earnings in some subjects have always been higher than in others, but the growth of consultancy may well increase existing differences within an academic community.

Extra-mural activities

The extra-mural activities of universities present a further range of tasks for academics. They have always been present to some degree in many universities, but are becoming more prominent with the increased proportion of students who are adult or part-time or both (Åhgren-Lange and Kogan 1992). They may encompass extra-mural teaching for adults seeking late entry to higher education or qualified personnel seeking continuing professional or work-related education which may, but need not, lead to the award of qualifications. They can take the form of part-time credit education, distance learning programmes, and learning in retirement programmes (Stern 1992). In France, centres for higher education can be inter-university in nature and offer counselling services and flexible hours. Finnish continuing education centres are thought to constitute 'a second wave' of the regionalisation of Finnish higher education, but, because they are somewhat isolated from the universities, it is thought that the universities should take on responsibility for teaching in them (Kivinen, Rinne and Hypponen 1992). Extra-mural activities can include work with outside organisations in a training or consultancy capacity, assistance to those seeking to develop economic activity or the development of the arts within the community. Again there is tension between the requirements of main-line teaching, research and scholarship and attention to the world outside the walls of the university. Outreach or extra-mural activities require an assessment of the needs of individuals and groups who do not form part of the university's registered population and the specification of teaching or applied research to their needs. Inevitably they suffer from status problems in an academic profession where improving research reputations is rated most highly (Åhgren-Lange and Kogan 1992).

Administration

Administration is a dichotomous set of tasks involving two different sets of structural characteristics. Almost all academics are involved in administration concerning the admission, assessment and examining of students and collective tasks on course construction and approval. These tasks are often regarded as burdensome chores undertaken with too little administrative help, and little recognition in the academic status competition. A second set of tasks concerns the management of institutions and has led to the creation of hierarchies of academic administrators who may be engaged in faculty or institutional management on a full or substantial part-time basis. Increasingly, a rector or vice-chancellor or director is now assisted not only by full-time professional administrators but also by deputy or assistant directors drawn from the academic ranks. Institutions have always required full-time administration. More now than before, national systems have required that they attend to such issues as quality and access, marketing and research policy which has given rise to new quasi-academic professions and role structures, a point to which we will return.

Leadership and service

In most universities it is no longer enough to be a committed teacher and/or researcher. There are expectations, legitimated in promotion and appointments criteria, that academic staff engage in a wide range of activities, some extending into the wider community. They have to contribute to course and departmental committees and initiatives, to involve themselves in faculty and eventually in institutional affairs. Some must demonstrate 'leadership' by initiating, coordinating and implementing policies and programmes. They may be impelled to be a prominent member of their professional or disciplinary association, engage in industry, government and community activities, liaise with schools and employers. Leadership and service have been particularly valued in the vocational sector which tends to be organised less collegially, more hierarchically, and where leadership was an important function of particular grades of academics.

The emphasis in some of the new universities on service and leadership in addition to research creates tensions between the cosmopolitan and local values. In order to get institutional recognition staff have to involve themselves in institutional and external affairs which can be to the detriment of more academic activities. At the same time, 'the opportunity to set one's own emphasis in academic work and to change it over a semester, a year, a career, has largely prevented burn-out and has thus enabled the university system to benefit from the multiple talents of academics' (Moses 1992a).

There is a danger that strong institutional leaders with a managerial bent will emphasise the entrepreneurial, short-term, commercial, community, industry or profession-linked programmes, whether in teaching or research, at the expense of some of the traditional values. These emphases demand commitment to institutional mission, faculty goals, departmental goals – the individual scholar is firmly placed into a group context.

Entrepreneurship

Relatively new but widespread throughout the member countries is the expectation that at least senior academic staff also possess entrepreneurial abilities and if not, develop these, to ensure for their academic unit an optimal share of resources and opportunities. This does not apply only to research and associated consultancy, but also and increasingly to finding and establishing 'market niches' for specific programmes of study and for particular student groups. Much of the lucrative market is found in other countries, requiring academics to be both culturally sensitive and entrepreneurial.

Implications

We have displayed the great range of tasks which must be performed by higher education as it moves into mass and universal education. Within each task itself there is great diversity, of level, of degree of theory and of application, of client group. It follows that faculties, taken across institutions certainly, but also within institutions, must be equally diverse in qualifications, approaches and motivations. At the same time as expertise and specialisation must be sustained, an institution must preserve cohesion and whole-system policies.

A new academic mandate is required. Because of the many pressures and forms of training and of enquiry with which higher education must compete, it is first necessary to define it in terms of what it is not. It is not simply training or consultancy or journalism, although academics may engage in those activities. Its distinguishing marks are the maintenance of traditional academic values – the disinterested search for the truth, and respect for logic, evidence and demonstrability. But the new mandate would seek to extend those virtues beyond classic research and scholarship towards more broadly based disciplined enquiry and to reformulations of the teaching task. Thus higher education teachers who are not engaged in research in the strict sense of the term can all the same apply scholarly forms of discipline to the application and testing of research findings in the world of application and action. Curriculum needs constant development.

The forms of organisational arrangements in the wider society call for reformulation of professionalism, to include greater responsiveness to the needs and views of clients.All of these enterprises are capable of being conceptualised and tested and thus form part of the range of disciplined enquiry. The academic should always be committed to the publication and dissemination of reformulations of these kinds. In this way higher education institutions can contribute to the creation of a knowledge-based society in which they take up the role of active, but expert, participants in concerns wider than the reformulation of academic disciplines.

The specific implications of our analysis of the changes in tasks are as follows:

- The tasks of academic staff have multiplied and their mandate has become less certain and needs to be redefined.

- The tensions between the various functions often are not acknowledged. These changes require both individuals and their institutions to make priorities between different activities.

- The use of such non-traditional methods as distance learning and information technology will become an increasingly important feature of higher education teaching.

- The need for closer relationships in both the curriculum and research with work undertaken outside higher education will call for the exercise of new skills on the part of higher education staff.

- These changes make it essential that there should be recruitment and staff development based on careful analyses of the requirements and strengths of both individuals and their departments.

- Decisions will have to be made about who does what. The proliferation of work may also justify the employment of a more varied and flexibly managed faculty group.This trend towards differentiation will reinforce managerial rather than collegial ways of working.

Chapter 4

The Academic Profession
Staffing Structures in Response
to New Demands

We have described some of the emerging characteristics of the academic profession and the increasing complexity of the academic task. Here we consider how far these changes are affecting the structure of academic appointments. Many of the changes noted here have been at work for a long time, probably from the onset of expansion in the 1960s. But the increased stress on numbers and limited resources brings them into greater prominence and in need of attention as current policy issues.

As we argue later, these developments have occurred casually and incrementally and need to be worked on systematically with a view to the needs of the system, of institutions and the individuals involved.

As we have seen in Chapter 2, the academic profession, inasmuch as it is meaningful to assume that such exists, is not monolithic. Here we take up four elements of differentiation: those of institutional status; those between sectors, and the nature of traditional staffing structures in contrast to newly emerging academic-related and para-academic structures.

Institutional statuses

In some countries, the vertical gradings within institutions are in some respects less important than horizontal stratification, that is, status differences between institutional types and institutions. The UK provides the clearest examples of this. Stratification is also explicit and powerful in the USA and other English-speaking systems whilst some other countries have made deliberate attempts to equalise statuses of universities although some of these also maintain a binary division between them and non-university institutions. Halsey demonstrates convincingly how esteem and academic power form a ladder starting with Oxbridge and going down through some of the colleges of London University, the major civic and 'greenfield' universities, the technological universities and the former public sector led by the former polytechnics. For example, academics surveyed expressed a preference for being an Oxbridge don rather than a professor in a well esteemed post-1960s university.

In the USA, rankings of academic departments and of institutions based on academic reputation are commonplace. The Carnegie classification of institutions is based on open and fixed criteria and, though not developed for this purpose, constitutes a hierarchy of institutions. Conditions of work, status, differentiation in the academic role, access to resources, and personal autonomy all vary within the different institution types.

Traditional structures and differences between sectors

Traditional structures remain strong although they differ between countries and between sectors within countries. In both Germany and Austria, professors are 'called' to a position on terms that are largely similar to those of a century ago.

In Germany, there were in 1991 over 54,000 university academics; of these more than a third were professors (of various categories), with another 45 per cent employed as *wissenschaftliche oder kunstlerische Mitarbeiter*, young scientists completing their PhD and assisting with research and teaching, many employed part-time (Göbbels-Dreyling 1993, see also Enders 1992). In the *Fachhochschulen* virtually all staff are called professor; there were 9600 such full-time positions in 1991, an increase of about 1700 over 1989.

Throughout Britain and many of the Commonwealth countries, the structure of lecturers, readers and professors was established under quite different historical circumstances. Academic staff from lecturer to professor basically have the same functions of teaching, research, and service/administration, and status is dependent on publicly acknowledged qualifications and expertise.

In the UK, in 1988–9, of 37,000 full-time academic staff in the 'old' universities 4000 were professors, 8500 were readers or senior lecturers, 25,000 were lecturers and 4500 were research staff. As in Australia, in recent years, assumptions about these gradings have been complicated by the award of professorial titles in the former polytechnics and colleges of higher education to teachers and administrators who would not have been so designated in the 'old' universities.

In Australia, in the universities in the Unified National System in 1992, there were more than 31,000 academic staff. Of these, 17.3 per cent were associate professors and professors; women constituted only about 10 per cent of the professoriate (DEET 1992). Despite the uniform nomenclature, significant differences in academic role and status are emerging based on the research prowess of both individuals and institutions. In the colleges, in contrast, lecturers, senior lecturers and principal lecturers had specific functions, i.e. leadership, and curriculum development and coordination are associated with positions.

In the recently created binary system in Finland, the universities have traditional structures, although with very few full professorial posts, whilst the polytechnics have no professorial posts and only one grade of teacher, although the intention is to recruit more staff with doctorates.

In the Netherlands, those holding traditional academic ranks, mostly tenured, with titles equivalent to lecturer, senior lecturer and professor, accounted for fewer than half of all academic staff in 1991. More than half of the academic staff held other titles, including teaching associates, research associates, and a new category, introduced in 1983, of research trainee. These positions, most of which are temporary, accounted for only about 16 per cent of academic staff a decade ago (Acherman 1993, Geurts, Maassen and Van Vught 1993).

The long-established pattern in North America is usually described as a career ladder, allowing progress from the bottom to the top: instructor, assistant professor, associate professor and professor.

Changes in academic role structure

Thus the core academic appointments are based on a structure of discrete titles and statuses that have long histories. But alongside these traditional structures there is a wide array of non-established academic and para-academic roles.

Work hitherto undertaken mainly by a permanent core staff is shared with growing numbers of temporary, part-time and ad hoc positions. Part-time appointments are used in most OECD countries; they usually have limited terms and have limited responsibilities. Their greater use reflects pressures on universities to achieve flexibility in making staff appointments and may relieve employers of responsibility for continued employment and makes savings in pensions and employer contribution liabilities.

These changes are largely a response to the added complexity and loads placed on higher education at a time when resource restrictions have made it difficult to appoint to more secure appointments many academics who in previous periods would have acquired tenure. At the same time, teaching or contributions to research can be bought in on a part-time basis from specialists in outside employment, and their employment may be wholly beneficial.

The need to cope with greater student numbers has also led to other forms of appointment, including those for teaching duties which carry no research expectations. In Sweden, the post of *lektor*, a full-time teacher, now apparently coming into disuse, was created in the 1960s for that purpose. There is also a category of 'adjunct' professor which allows those with professional qualifications to spend 20 per cent of their time teaching at universities. These appointments, used frequently elsewhere, too, without formal categorisation, have been developed to encourage transfer of knowledge between universities and industry, and are primarily financed by industrial firms and other external sources (Castro 1993). Categories of trainee continue to exist in many countries; this is an apprentice-like position, variously labelled, in which they carry out such academic tasks as those of teaching or research assistants, while also conducting their own doctoral research.

Universities have increasingly created para-academic roles to carry out a routinised version of some portion of the academic role or in other ways provide support to the academic programme. This includes the role of academic adviser, for example, which in some large American universities was created to relieve professors of the burden of academic advising.

Another factor is that grants and contracts became more prominent in university resourcing in the 1960s in the USA and UK and
fully established throughout the 1970s, and as a result universities
appointed increasing numbers of non-tenured full-time researchers.

Roles have so proliferated that in the United States, as in many
other countries, neither the 'ladder' image nor other logical categories accurately depict the confusion of academic positions found
in practice. The categories for most data reporting on academic
staff lag behind reality, and offer simplified images that obscure
important new developments in academic staffing. As we argue
later, these developments have occurred casually and incrementally and need to be worked on systematically with a view to the
needs of the system, of institutions and the individuals involved.

Such changes in the structure of academic appointments are
affected by specific circumstances in each country, including differences in the labour market, in political strengths, in cultural
values and in the structure of the higher education system itself.
Some countries have largely maintained their traditional categories even though actual responsibilities have been modified to
provide better opportunities for certain categories of staff. In Bel-
gium, special mid-level appointments have been offered as a way
to give improved salary and status to some who felt blocked for
promotion (Absalom and Sutton 1992).

Only a few attempts have been made to develop a new 'map'
or diagram of academic staffing (cf. Enders 1992) and typically
have thus far led to octopus-like designs, with many separate
tentacles in place of a clear and defined structure, with connections
between different groups.

The original structure of a hierarchy of permanent staff had a
kind of logic which still persists. It assumed that universities
should be staffed by faculty able to withstand external political and
sectarian pressures by virtue of their tenure and status. It assumed,
too, that newcomers need to go through a period of rigorous
training before being admitted to tenure, and that there will be
rigorous assessment before they occupy publicly recognised academic gradings. Thus lecturers, or their equivalents, were assumed
to be fully capable of teaching and research on their own initiative
and professors had a publicly recognisable claim to leadership in
their areas of scholarship and research. These firm underpinnings

to a system that still lays claim to authority as it certifies and advises the rest of the world will remain necessary. But there remains the problem of the relationship between the core and the non-tenured staff.

Part-time faculty

The firmness of established structures has led to a casual treatment of many now employed in higher education. Universities need to be able to employ part-timers because they require particular forms of expertise that only those with an outside employment base can provide. They also constitute a low cost resource at a time of financial stringency, or enable universities to overcome other employment restrictions. For example, in Germany, a temporary category of *Tutoren*, postgraduate students to take responsibility for seminars and tutorial groups, was introduced as a partial response to restrictions on the use of permanent posts.

A recent study in Canada, which refers to part-time faculty as 'hidden academics' (the Dutch call them 'throw away academics'), offers unusual insight into this little-understood status (Rajagopal and Farr 1992). Part-time appointments are extensive, accounting for more than a third of all academic staff positions in Canada. Actual use varies widely by institution; however, in Ontario, part-time faculty as a percentage of full-time faculty range from 10 per cent to 130 per cent across 17 institutions.

Disciplinary differences are strong as well. In the Canadian study, part-time appointments were made most often in the arts and humanities, and much less often in the traditional research-dominant fields of the sciences. In other situations, part-timers are employed in fields where the linkages to other employment sectors are strong. In Spain, for example, part-time appointments are found most often in faculties of law, economics, and business. Large numbers of part-time appointments are also reported by Spain's technical colleges, the *escuelas technicas superiores*.

The Canadian study also demonstrates that part-time appointments are no longer an aberration, a limited or transitory response to short-term needs. Rather, part-time appointments have grown to the extent that they have become a critical element in university financing, '... a relatively inexpensive teaching resource ...' that has become '... an integral part of academe ...'. In Quebec, about 40 per cent of all courses were offered by part-timers; in Ontario in

1987–88, part-timers accounted for at least one-fifth of total teaching.

Cost-savings are a major incentive for the use of part-time appointments in Canada. Because part-timers are paid stipends on a much lower wage basis than full-timers, and are provided many fewer benefits, their 'unit costs' are much lower. Rajagopal and Farr estimated that, in Ontario, part-time salaries were about 8 per cent of total academic salaries, even though part-timers accounted for a third of all academics. Put differently, the average salary of one full-time position provided the equivalent of four full-time positions when it was used for part-time appointments.

This Canadian study, especially its attention to wage differentials, provides concrete evidence of the 'outsider' status of part-time academics. A substantial pay differential also exists in other countries. In the United States, one estimate is that part-timers are paid 25 to 35 per cent less than full-time faculty (Gappa 1984). Other countries, including the Netherlands, offer remuneration that is proportionally more akin to what is provided for full-time positions. For example, staff working a four day week may receive 80 per cent of full salary and a proportionate amount of pension, vacation and other rights. Access to fringe benefits also varies across countries but, generally, part-time appointments have fewer benefits. In Canada, benefit coverage costs 4.5 per cent of part-time salaries, but 12 to 13 per cent of full-time salaries; certain health benefits, vacation days and other leave are not available to part-time faculty (Rajagopal and Farr 1992).

Apart from differentials in pay and benefits, other aspects of part-time appointments reinforce their peripheral, or outsider, status. In many countries, part-timers have little access to opportunities for professional development. The Canadian study documented that part-timers had very little access to support for research activity, whether as research leave, training in research skills, or travel support for conferences, or to training and assistance with their instructional skills (Rajagopal and Farr 1992).

Most often, part-time appointees have limited access to such basic support services as telephones, secretarial assistance, or office space. Typically, too, they have limited interaction with full-time academics, even in the same department, and might not take part in meetings, whether departmental or university-wide.

The justification for such differential treatment has long been the view that persons on part-time appointments are temporary employees or a small part of the overall workforce. If this remains true at some universities and in some countries, it is no longer the case for many OECD countries. Documentation is spotty, precisely because universities have not actively monitored this category of academic employee, but the available data point to a sizeable and increasingly stable 'underclass' of part-timers. In California, records compiled by faculty unions have shown that large numbers of part-time faculty teaching in the California State University system have held a succession of one-year appointments continuously for ten to fifteen years. In order to assemble an adequate income, some of these part-timers teach at several universities in the system during the same term; they have been called 'freeway fliers', needing to travel heavily on the freeways in order to get to all of their classes. Part-time and short-term contract appointees are also prevalent in Australia and experience similar problems.

The extensive use of part-timers who suffer these disadvantages also creates problems for full-time staff. Kalkum found that many were teaching beginning students in the basic subjects. While part-time teachers' subject competence may be adequate, they cannot be expected to have the educational orientation and experience of full-time faculty, even if the latter's knowledge of educational processes has only come through teaching experience. They cannot participate in the full work of a teacher and because they may work to specific hours will not be available for contact outside class with students or for pastoral or administrative work. Paradoxically, therefore, the full-timers may find that they have less time for teaching and research because there are fewer of them to shoulder general duties. Heads of departments must cope with the increased administration created by the employment of larger numbers of staff working in fragmented ways. It is more difficult to sustain cohesion and continuity with a floating population of part-time and temporary staff.

The widespread use of professionally qualified staff and research students raises the question of whether the teaching–research nexus, so dear to many faculty, has any reality for students. In practice, many institutions employ teaching staff who are not active researchers, and some of them would not have had any research training.

Full-time contract researchers

The growth of contract and grant aided research has given rise to an enlarged population of full-time researchers, on time-limited contracts. They have no formal teaching responsibilities, though they might be drawn into them; in the UK it is not uncommon for them to have student contact of up to six hours a week in term time. They are usually funded entirely by external funds on limited-term contracts. Since the 1960s many universities have employed increasing numbers but though their position was not as favourable as those of tenured staff they at least had some prospect of being proposed for tenurial posts, and contract research was an ante-chamber to tenure for some. They also had the prospect of reasonably long-term contracts, with some chance of renewal. Some were able to stay fully employed in the same institution for most of their working lives, and some were given professorial title. In Denmark, a special, fixed-term position of research professor was created in the technical and scientific disciplines, with the expectation that many of those in this position would receive professorial appointments eventually.

If their position was nevertheless that of second class citizens in those more favourable times it has now deteriorated considerably. There are more of them, but on increasingly shorter contracts which have to be competed for more vigorously. The projects may have to be more attuned to sponsors' immediate needs without much room for personal development. They have never had any right to sabbatical leave; the problem now is more that of continuous and satisfying employment.

It has, indeed, been argued (Jackson 1990) that a shift to non-tenurial staffing is both likely and desirable. In the UK, research selectivity is leading to the creation of centres of excellence funded for research. These, it is thought, might provide a good employment base for researchers who can rely on continuity of employment opportunities, but not permanencies from centres funded on a long-term basis. So far that thought has yet to become reality. Nor is it clear what will happen to contract researchers in well established centres when or if they cease to be productive.

Full-time temporary teachers

Titles and definitions vary widely but, in many OECD countries, an increasingly significant part of the work-force includes persons in full-time positions who have temporary, short-term contracts In Greece, non-tenured posts, termed 'special teaching staff', are allowed to provide instruction in only certain subjects, including foreign languages, drama, music and physical education.

Many holding full-time limited-term contracts have no explicit expectation for continued appointment. They may hold two- to five-year contracts that are renewable and that, indeed, are often renewed; however, there is always uncertainty. In France, for example, positions as *professeur associé* are a fixed-term appointment of three years, although renewable, that were designed especially for non-academic professionals. Others do not have uncertainty; instead, they hold limited-term contracts that cannot be renewed. The Spanish government permits a limited number of non-permanent teaching appointments, of no more than two or three years in length.

These full-time non-tenured appointments account for at least 10 per cent of the American professoriate today. They are used by most universities as another way to offer staffing flexibility, but are less prevalent than part-time appointments. Full-time non-tenure appointments are especially found at institutions located outside of metropolitan areas, where there is a limited availability of persons for part-time appointments.

A recent US study of 'non-tenure' or 'non-tenure-track' appointments (Chronister, Baldwin and Bailey 1992) shows that many of the marks of peripheral status that were described for part-timers also are characteristic of persons in these full-time non-tenure positions. Compared with other academics, they are paid less, have fewer opportunities to engage in research, carry heavier teaching loads, and have significantly less involvement in departmental or university-wide faculty meetings and committees. Despite their full-time status and appropriate credentials, they were not being encouraged in their development of an academic career.

Growth of managerial and administrative functions

Differentiation within academic staffing is matched by the growth and elaboration of those responsible for maintaining the total institution. Universities have always been run on diarchical lines incorporating managerial and collegial lines of authority (Moodie and Eustace 1974, Becher and Kogan 1992). The head of the university – rector, president or vice-chancellor – leads a system which is in principle collegial inasmuch as most academic decision making is either individual or sanctioned by committees of academics. Academic decision making, and linkage with the managerial line of authority, is serviced by deans of faculties and heads of departments. They are in a somewhat ambiguous position inasmuch as they have uncertain managerial powers to administer the system other than through the consent of their colleagues, from whom they are recruited and to whom they usually return. Part of the drive towards managerialism has been to invest them with clearer managerial authority (e.g. Jarratt 1985, Lockwood and Davies 1985). These moves are the result of the increased demands on academics to meet demands for evaluation and defined quality, to reorganise the delivery of the curriculum, and to compete for resources. They create extra loads on senior academics and, for some, a change of role. Such changes were heralded in the UK and Australia in the former non-university sector where central institutional direction was always more likely.

As the functions of academic management have grown so have those of the professional administrators who have always constituted the second line of management and administration deriving authority ultimately from the head of the institution. In some systems, however, rectors are elected by academic staff whilst the directors are appointed by the government. Administrators' functions include the administration of rules throughout the institution, even when these are generated by academics, the maintenance of financial allocations and controls, the maintenance of the personnel and physical resources of the institution and the servicing of the academic decision-making system.

Both more central control and devolution create more work at the institutional level. Cuts in resources, the changing relationships with central government and the increased number of students have caused the workload and power of non-academic, but professional, administration to grow. Within administration there is growing specialisation in such areas as finance and personnel. In each of these roles, as in academic work, balances have to be struck between different goals.

Increased pressure for institutional development and control, too, has led to the employment of officers in a new range of tasks that derive in part from the persuasions of public policy rather than academic development. In the United Kingdom and in some other European countries, roles such as quality assurance officer, academic planner or staff development officer have emerged during the last decade. In North America, institutional researchers and planners are widely prevalent employment categories, and European universities are following the same patterns. American universities also support the employment of many persons in associate dean and assistant dean positions to carry out a wide variety of tasks in support of academic programmes.

The balance of power between academic and non-academic management has changed: one leading UK university registrar is reported as saying, after the first and most severe round of cuts, 'Now there is no academic veto.' Good institutional working requires cooperation and communication between faculty and administration which is not always evident. It might also lead to a blending of roles as more administration falls to academics. The combination of and balance between support and control functions, essential for good administration, are difficult to achieve. Many issues require full-time and expert application unlikely to be undertaken willingly by academics and good understanding of the institutional tasks that must be performed would enable better team working between the different groups.

Implications

Absalom and Sutton (1992) have pointed to delayed advancement prospects for junior staff, reduced satisfaction with traditional teaching and research roles when entrepreneurial and consulting roles gain status, and changes in status distinctions occasioned by the team characteristics of externally funded research. As they point out, most institutional responses have, in general, been to '... seek minimalist amelioration of existing structures or temporary adjustments...'.

The foregoing analysis suggests, however, that the proliferation of staffing categories is not anomalous or transitory. Rather, the shifting categories represent attempts to respond to several fundamental forces which are buffeting institutions. These include the conduct of large-scale research projects and sometimes far-reaching collaborative relationships with industry. Handling expanding enrolment and instructional requirements without a parallel increase in staffing resources is another reality of higher education administration today. In some countries, too, institutions can not meet these problems effectively because they are hampered by civil service regulations which may get in the way of structural changes.

Certain aspects of the shift in the categories of staffing call into question the viability of the academic profession. Because the positions that have been growing in number occupy peripheral status, there is a prospect of a strong cleavage between two tiers of academic staff, those with status and reputations versus those with uncertain status, considerable teaching responsibility, and constraints on their ability to develop their own scholarly interests. They may develop quite distinct identities. They may become openly antagonistic. This relationship will hardly give junior staff the kind of experience needed to qualify for more senior positions.

These are issues which need to be tackled at several levels. National authorities may have to shift legal restrictions in order to give institutions more flexibility. Institutions should think more actively about their human resources and in the interest both of justice and of good functioning consider how to align the conditions and contributions of the different academic staff groups. The unions, too, must face the facts that tasks and roles are becoming more rather than less unitary, and that there are matters affecting many of their members which need to be analysed and presented to institutional management. There are, therefore, several policy issues for the long-run strength and vitality of higher education:

- The traditional structures served to create cohesion among academics of different status, offering a sense of shared interests. But the sense of cohesion is likely to be eroded as status and other differentials increase, especially between staff with permanent appointments and those on temporary or part-time contracts.

- It is no longer sensible to speak of a single academic profession, but there are a large number of professional groups working in universities each with their own tasks. These configurations need to be recognised and regularised.

- A caste distinction is emerging between 'have' and 'have-not' groups. An underclass is appearing, with limited prospects for advancement or employment stability. The conditions of full- and part-time temporary researchers and teachers should be specified in terms of requisite functions, appropriate conditions of work and of prospects. The concepts of collegium should be capable of extension to all who help service the academic system. At the same time, the contribution of part-timers to teaching and research recruited from external forms of employment should be recognised.

- The long-term question is whether the academic profession can sustain itself under today's new staffing conditions; this question will have increased urgency in the late 1990s, as large numbers of senior professors begin to retire. There is every prospect, in most OECD countries, that efficiency pressures will continue and that academic staffing needs will be increasingly seen in managerial terms.

- Higher education needs a pool of well-trained and appropriately motivated persons capable of moving into the upper levels of academic life. Under new staffing conditions, the 'reserve pool' is unlikely to be sufficient in size and properly prepared. Junior staff positions do not offer appropriate experience and career challenges as preparation for more demanding roles. Institutions must therefore address the staff development needs of this group.

- Much will depend on the willingness of the large cadre of junior staff to continue their affiliation with universities.There should be review of their contributions, both in monetary rewards and prospects and in the more intrinsic benefits associated with university life.

- Increased differentials and tensions among top-level academic ranks may create new difficulties in securing collaboration across departmental boundaries.

- Unions representing staff might be expected to develop agendas that face more strongly these growing status differentials.

- A thoroughgoing appraisal of these developments is needed. To have a secure core does not entail the existence of an underprivileged and swollen outer circle of teachers and researchers. Some approximation between tenure and non-tenurial posts must therefore be made, and their respective roles fully analysed.

Chapter 5

Policies and Practices
Qualifications and Staff Development

Functions

From consideration of the changing staffing structures we turn to consider how the functions of different sectors and institutions may be expected to lead to different academic work patterns and qualifications. The analysis of different practices will help determine fits between tasks, structure and qualifications. We can then consider how they might be reformulated for future patterns of work. In tackling these matters we follow the following sequence of issues: the functions of higher education and how they affect career structures; entry qualifications; preparation and selection for academic careers; and the development of staff once admitted to employment.

We begin by reminding the reader of the wide range of functions noted in earlier chapters. These are well brought together in the 1987 OECD report, *Universities under Scrutiny*, which listed ten functions of universities:

1. general, post-secondary education
2. pursuit of research and scholarship
3. assist in fulfilling the manpower needs of the 'expert society'
4. high level specialised education and training
5. strengthening the competitive edge of the economy
6. act as screening mechanism
7. avenue for social mobility
8. services to the region and immediate community
9. act as exemplars of certain national policies
10. performance of leadership roles.

We will return later to discuss the extent to which faculty feel responsible for seeing that their knowledge and skills are adequate to meet these demands. It is however obvious that the multiplicity of functions must be taken into account by management and faculty as they consider the selection and preparation of staff.

Structures

As we have seen, academic careers differ from country to country: entry points, career paths, and employment status vary. The differences are partly due to the different notion of academic work at different stages of an academic career. The English-speaking systems tend to have similar provisions for progression by merit, although they vary in the length of the academic career ladder. However, in many countries academic careers differ between the higher education sectors.

The USA model with a tenure track from assistant via associate to full professor is only now being implemented in Australia, though not yet by using this nomenclature. Until recently, in Britain, Australia and New Zealand university lecturers could be promoted to senior lecturer and reader/associate professor, but chairs (professorships) and the entry to the career position of lecturer were normally only available if a position was advertised. In the college system, in Australia, for example, promotion on merit was only possible where a position was available.

In Germany, the professor alone has the right to assess theses *(Prüfungsrecht)*. This leads to unofficial involvement of more junior colleagues and a perception of being overworked on the part of both senior and junior staff. With many of the tasks being accepted unofficially to gain experience in research or teaching, there is less opportunity for professional maturing and experimentation in teaching, or preparedness to innovate. In Australian colleges, in contrast, lecturers, senior lecturers and principal lecturers have had specific functions, i.e. leadership, curriculum development and coordination are associated with positions. But in universities in the English-speaking world, academic staff from lecturer to professor basically have the same functions of teaching, research and service/administration, and status is dependent on publicly acknowledged qualifications and expertise.

Entry qualifications

The entry point to the academic profession varies in the different countries. In the sciences generally, doctoral or post-doctoral qualifications provide an entry, although many doctoral students are already part of the profession by virtue of their part-time teaching role. There are, however, many entry points unlike in other professions. One may reach the pinnacle by moving in laterally, partly by the acknowledgment of 'equivalent' qualifications and experience.

While not all systems have a hierarchy of graduate degrees, others do. In the English-speaking countries generally a PhD is seen as being the terminal degree, and in disciplines where the PhD would be expected qualification, i.e. in the sciences, all faculty within the academic hierarchy would have it. In other systems there is a differentiation in qualifications between the professoriate and other academic ranks.

In Britain, the importance placed on a first class honours degree has been somewhat diminished because doctoral degrees are increasingly an entry qualification to the academic profession. Success in the academic profession, however, is still somewhat determined by academic pedigree. Halsey noted that more academics who held the highest academic positions, professorships, had a doctorate from Oxford or Cambridge than other academic ranks, and that the quality of first degrees held by faculty corresponded to the status of the institution (Halsey 1992).

The level of formal qualifications needed at entry point differs between sectors. Sectorial differences in formal qualifications have impact on academic career opportunities and on mobility between various sectors. In the USA, where PhDs are accepted as the entry qualification, the values and the status of the doctorate-granting universities often have become dominant and influence practice and priorities in academic work even in those institutions where they are inappropriate (Lynton and Elman 1987).

Formal qualifications are important, and a number of staffing policy studies assume that only persons with doctorates are potential academics although this assumption is being challenged by policy makers. In Canada, a recent study (Davidson 1991) noted that by 1988 nearly three quarters of all faculty held a PhD. However, an analysis of new appointments showed that less than half of the appointments were appointed immediately after receiving their doctorate (Davidson 1991).

In Australia, a similar analysis (Sloan *et al.* 1990) started with the same premise but was heavily criticised by the government department that had commissioned the study. Indeed, a subsequent analysis of degree qualifications of academic staff found much lower percentages of academics holding PhDs: about 57 per cent of university staff in 1990 held doctoral degrees, and 28 per cent of staff in the former college sector (Australian Higher Education Council 1991). In the (former) polytechnics in the UK, too, fewer staff held a PhD.

In systems where there is an academic career ladder, notably in the English-speaking systems, it is possible to gain junior positions and to enjoy full-time pay while involved in furthering competencies in research. Postdoctoral fellowships and tutor positions are such examples. In the Netherlands special positions have been created to allow young researchers to complete a doctoral dissertation in a reasonable time on full pay. In Germany, faculty appointed to a chair or another professorship in a university generally are expected to have a Dr habil, a higher doctorate based on a dissertation or a set of already published research. The concentration on *Habilitation* work in some disciplines keeps junior academics in contract positions longer, and appointment to a professorship is a big jump in status, independence and resources.

Sectorial differences in entry qualifications

In Germany, the Dr habil is awarded following a PhD, and virtually all university professors have a PhD. In institutions with an explicit vocational orientation, e.g. *Fachhochschulen*, colleges of advanced education and institutes of technology, polytechnic-specific non-degree qualifications are deemed to be of PhD or Habilitation level. Applicants for professorships in *Fachhochschulen* need to demonstrate their ability to conduct independent scholarly work; many do this not by undertaking PhD studies but by presenting praxis as scholarly work. However, there has been a dramatic increase (from 41% to 73%) in the proportion of professors appointed in the *Fachhochschulen* with a PhD over a period 1970–1982/4, and a clear trend towards more applicants for positions with a doctorate (Kalkum 1989).

The same phenomenon of 'credentialism' is evident in Australia and the USA and is both a reflection of the availability of PhD graduates and the knowledge demands made on academic staff.

As noted above, in Australia, until the recent demise of the binary line (Moses 1991a), academic staff in universities (equivalent to UK universities and North American research universities) held significantly more often research degrees than their counterparts in the advanced education sector, while faculty in the colleges had more industry/praxis experience (Moses and Ramsden 1991). This also applies to UK (former) polytechnics. Clearly, then, the formal qualifications expected of faculty at entry point to the academic profession reflect the function of the sector.

Praxis versus research qualifications

The value placed on formal research qualifications in the university sector and of praxis experience in polytechnics, *Fachhochschulen* and colleges has implications for academic careers. Research credentials enable faculties to engage in research – independently or as responsible members of a group. If faculties do not engage in research it may be argued that their skills and knowledge become antiquated and at best redundant, at worst dangerous to the student's education who may be misled.

Practical experience prior to appointment to a professorship is required but professional practice or consultancy is also expected during the appointment in all institutions that provide primarily vocational training, and in university professional courses. Some faculties continue to apply their knowledge in professional practice by consulting and mission-oriented research and contacts with industry and consultancies. Where practical experience qualifies applicants for professorial positions it needs to be scholarly in order to be equivalent to scientific qualifications. In German *Fachhochschulen*, professors have to provide evidence of special achievements in the application or development of scientific knowledge and methods over a period of five years, of which three at least have to be external to higher educational institutions (Kalkum 1989).

Insistence on experience in the vocational sector is based on the assumption that it will assure a praxis-relevant curriculum and teaching, and possibly continued links with industry. Kalkum (1989), however, makes the valid point that most praxis experience is specific, not generalisable, easily dated and, if not reflected on, will not benefit students' education. Equally, if professors, appointed because of their practical experience, project without reflection and revision their own norms and orientations based on their specific experience, they may do neither justice to the learning goals of the course nor the specific group of students. Practical experience may not be always complemented by understanding of the scientific foundation of one's discipline and its relation to praxis. If practical experience is not permeated by theory, students may well receive a limited – and limiting – understanding of praxis. Professionals who draw on knowledge-in-action (Schön 1987) need to learn to reflect on this, so that they can translate it and integrate it with theory and curricula.

Disciplinary differences in entry qualifications

As noted below, there are discipline-based academic labour markets. They require different formal qualifications for entry to the academic professions or success in it. Recent Australian data showed significant differences in highest qualification held by faculty between various disciplines or fields of study across all higher education institutions (Australian Higher Education Council 1991). While the newer professions have a relatively low proportion of members with PhDs, there is a general trend towards acceptance of the doctorate as the terminal degree of faculty regardless of discipline.

In Germany, Holtkamp, Fischer-Bluhm and Huber (1986) conducted a large-scale investigation of young scientists at universities. They found large disciplinary differences in the importance of graduate study and postdoctoral study for academic work. A PhD is a prerequisite for an academic career in law in German universities, though the thesis itself may be, but not always is, seen by experts as a contribution to knowledge and the research is rarely embedded in larger research projects. On the other hand, the contribution to the development of the discipline for the *Habilitation* is high. There are wide variations in the other study areas on the extent to which a PhD or *Habilitation* is required for academic advancement, and this is a function of the nature of scholarship and research, and the degree of praxis required in the discipline or field.

Preparation for the academic profession

The academic profession is unique in the way recruits are prepared for academic work, particularly when we compare it with the preparation for professional practice in the older learned professions. Both lawyers and medical practitioners undergo an extensive training/education programme which is shared in its core by all medical or law students. It is only after graduation and accreditation by the relevant professional bodies that medical students can specialise following more study and specialist registrations. Academic staff, in contrast, have little in common in their professional preparation. Some of the processes and minimum standards are shared, but the outcomes are very specific.

Academic staff in all countries generally hold an academic qualification at least at the same level as they are teaching. Much of the rest is country, sector and discipline specific and has been changing over time as well.

In considering qualifications, knowledge and skills for academic work we need to consider basically three variables, and each within its national context: (1) the point of entry to the academic profession; (2) in which discipline the appointment is; and (3) in which institution type the appointment is. The discussion of these variables is related to broad academic functions. Therefore, first of all we need to examine academic work, and the knowledge and skills needed in order to carry it out.

Academic work

The core functions of academic staff are teaching and research, complemented by service to the institution, to the professions, and to society. The knowledge and skills may be obtained during pre-academic education or employment, on-the-job concurrently with academic work through separate programmes or through on-going development, or in time-out arrangements such as sabbaticals. These have been called the initiation phase, induction phase and in-the-service phase of preparation (Cahill 1991).

In UK universities, disciplinary expertise validated by formal research qualifications (PhD) and research record as evidenced by publications and/or reputation tend to be the paramount criteria for appointments beyond the entry level. Scholarly expertise differs by levels, but there is a general expectation that academic staff are qualified for and actually engaged in research, in accordance with universities' missions.

In vocationally oriented institutions, there is a different hierarchy of knowledge, skills and experience; emphasis is on teaching programmes and praxis. Hence applicants' contribution to the teaching programme chiefly requires broad familiarity with the field of study rather than specialised knowledge. In contrast to research expertise which in universities qualifies academics for teaching as well as research, in vocational sectors staff are teaching 'received wisdom' within an applied context. Universities, too, of course, have vocationally oriented courses and here both higher degree and practical experience are seen as valuable qualifications.

In some institutions, certainly for senior positions, leadership and managerial ability are stressed in addition to research success. This emphasis was until recently quite specific to the vocational sector both in Britain and Australia, but has become part of the changing culture in higher education.

As noted above, praxis experience in itself has limited value unless it is reflected and integrated with theoretical and methodological advances in the field. Many institutions in many countries provide faculty with the opportunity to engage in consultancy and praxis; usually the individual academic staff member decides how this experience is then integrated into the curriculum and used for forging links with the professions/industry.

Wherever we have clear distinctions between and within institutions on the basis of pure and applied courses, e.g. between physics and engineering, sociology and social work, economics and commerce, and between basic research and applied research and/or consultancy, we are likely to find academics of very different orientations. Faculty with a disciplinary orientation, active in research and publication/creative endeavours, tend to be part of an international community of scholars, and to derive their self-esteem and rewards through the recognition which it affords them. These 'cosmopolitans' (Gouldner 1957) are mainly found in the universities which emphasise advancement and creation of knowledge.

In the non-university sector, many staff have a different orientation in line with the functions of these institutions: they are 'locals'. Their loyalty is to the institution, to the professions demonstrated by providing vocational training for a particular student body, and to the community and the region.

In *Fachhochschulen*, Kalkum (1989) notes, professors are not primarily oriented to the discipline but to the profession – their own or their graduates'. This is exacerbated by emphasis on teaching and professional functions, expressed in high teaching loads and expectations of practical work. Similar to their colleagues in Australian colleges, faculty do not have an explicit research function. This in itself weakens the allegiance to one's home discipline. As a consequence colleagues from this sector tend to be at the margin of the scientific community. This is borne out by research data (Moses and Ramsden 1991) which showed that academics in the college sector participated to a much smaller extent in peer review and interaction than their colleagues in corresponding disciplines in the university sector.

One way of overcoming the theory–praxis tension is by cooperative research or research training. The Australian Research Council has made available scholarships for PhD study in industry, but supervised in academia; research fellowships, too, have been created to be taken up on industry projects. As these schemes have not yet been evaluated it remains to be seen whether the integration of theory and praxis can be achieved this way. The proliferation of masters' programmes based on coursework with a research component may well contribute more, as the graduate students are generally professionals who choose for their research praxis-relevant issues and thus bring to it their own experience, and analytical skills to their praxis.

Preparation for the research function

Research may be described as the scholarship of discovery, of advancement of knowledge and of understanding. Academic staff are systematically trained in research in their own higher degree studies. Socialisation into the disciplinary culture occurs in the interaction with the discipline and colleagues during doctoral and postdoctoral study. In the pure disciplines it is through research study that one obtains a professional identity as physicist, historian or sociologist.

Students are not only socialised into discovery and advancement of knowledge, but also gain experience in the scholarship of integration through advanced coursework and literature reviews.

The scholarship of integration may be practised through teaching and writing.

Preparation for research has been synonymous with preparation for a career as university teacher. It normally takes place in universities, in institutions with a research mission, with resources and faculty with expertise and involvement in research, indeed where the central function of research and preparation for research is acknowledged in promotion and tenure procedures, and in formal and informal hierarchies. In most systems only some types of institution may grant doctoral degrees – here the research training is concentrated and the professoriate reproduces itself.

The doctorate is the admission to membership in the specific scientific community, a certification that the paradigms and practices, conventions and communication patterns have been internalised. The training can be obtained either through formalised research degree study as occurs in some systems, e.g. notably USA, UK, Australia and Japan, or as part of a 'traditional scientific apprenticeship' (Blume 1986) as used to operate in Norway and until recently in the Netherlands. In Germany, both professional research training and apprenticeship models are functioning. In engineering, for example, the doctorate was seen more as a by-product than the primary goal of research undertaken (Holtkamp *et al.* 1986).

Enrolment in graduate studies has increased dramatically over the past few years, though mostly in coursework programmes (OECD 1987b), and in most countries there has been ensuing concern about the organisation and purpose of graduate studies and their perceived inefficiencies: number of graduates not related to labour market needs; high drop-out rates; long completion times (Smith 1985, OECD 1987b, Becher *et al.* 1993).

Driven by instrumentalist concerns, regularisation of study lengths, generally across the disciplines without regard to students' educational intentions or the differences in the nature of research, was instituted in Australia and in Britain. In the Netherlands, humanities departments resisted 'the notion of formalised PhD-type training as being something other than and far from their conception of an apprenticeship in scholarship' (OECD 1987b). In the UK it is proposed that all science and technology students will first complete a one year's master's course and that only a limited and selected group should be financed to proceed to doctoral studies. This has been stipulated without regard to whether all disciplines perceive a need for a prerequisite year of course work. Other proposals include training for researchers in management of research and induction into the ways of industry (White Paper 1993). We note in Chapter 6 that systematic policies are lacking on the supply, recruitment and employment in relation to competing labour markets of those with advanced qualifications.

The limitation in length of candidature comes at a time when knowledge explosion, differentiation, specialisation and the need for more interdisciplinary links make more demands on graduate students. Questions are being asked about the purpose and scope of research training even for those entering an academic career, for example, whether it is desirable for a student to spend the entire academic career in a single laboratory where in-depth knowledge of techniques is acquired at the expense of breadth in the discipline. Advanced coursework is advocated in addition to the acquisition of specialised knowledge.

In sciences in particular doctoral training usually precedes full-time employment in any sector of higher education. In sciences, where graduate study tends to be more structured, giving less scope to the student for independent work, originality, and responsibility for the different stages of a research project, a period of postdoctoral work is usually required before gaining a teaching–research position.

In many other areas doctoral qualifications may be obtained during employment. Indeed, in Australia, after the demise of the binary line the federal government made available $5 million per annum for six years for academic development; in the first year (1991) four-fifths was used for upgrading qualifications and research skills of faculty from the former college sector. Clearly, faculty themselves not only thought it necessary to acquire formal qualifications equal to those of their university colleagues, but also valued the intellectual stimulation, rigour and disciplinary knowledge associated with advanced course work and research degree study.

While research training occurs more or less systematically, certainly as an intentional preparation for the research function, other aspects of research are mostly left to chance learning (Becher *et al.* 1993). Research management, writing grant applications, budgeting, writing for publication, liaising with the media, are all learnt by modelling successful colleagues or by trial-and-error. Commercialisation of one's own and students' research findings poses additional problems. In several countries, including Britain and Australia, however, institutions and funding bodies now assist faculty with these tasks by written materials, courses and feedback. And many universities have companies and guidelines which address intellectual property and commercialisation issues.

In France, the new title of *habilitation à diriger des recherches* has become the necessary qualification for aspirants to the post of professor and also for supervisors of doctoral students. Supervisors of doctoral students need to be active and productive in original research and demonstrate their capacity to develop a research strategy and to supervise research students (OECD 1987b).

Preparation for the teaching function

Most academics become experts in their field of study by mastering its knowledge base and techniques, its discourse and structures, its modes of inquiry and conventions of communication. They gain this expertise through advanced study and application or through professional practice, and they stay expert by continuous engagement with their field of learning and practice.

Teaching at tertiary level at its best requires not only a high level of competence and expertise in the discipline and/or relevant professional experience, but also developed communication and interpersonal skills. Students not only learn academic content and intellectual and practical skills, but learn from faculty as professional role models. They learn to think, argue, define and solve problems, to develop research proposals, evaluate appropriate methodologies and to analyse data by observing, following and evaluating what their professors do.

Teachers therefore need to model for students a commitment to scholarly values, to life-long learning, to professional and personal growth through critical reflection and self-evaluation, to accountability for one's own professional activities, and a responsible and ethical practice of one's profession.

As scholars, university teachers hope to instil in their students a love for their discipline and for learning, a sense of progress towards competence and maturity, and excitement for the opportunities each graduate will have to contribute to society. The researchers among the academics hope to inspire students to take research courses and even choose research careers, but all academics would instil in students a respect for research and the ability to question it.

Students expect and value in university teachers competence in their areas, effective communication of their knowledge and experience, interest and enthusiasm for their subject, concern and respect for students as persons, and a commitment to facilitating learning for each student (Moses 1985). All university teachers have a professional responsibility to develop, teach and assess their subjects in such a way that students, regardless of their background or characteristics, can demonstrate that they have learned in accordance with the subject aims.

Where do academic staff receive training for this complex set of tasks? The scholarship of teaching, which includes representation, but also integration and application of knowledge, is mostly learnt on the job.

In this way teaching higher education in contrast to research is unprofessional: there are no agreed standards, no body of knowledge and skills that neophytes have to master before they are allowed to practice, no peer review, no accountability (although as we saw in Chapter 2 attempts are being made in several countries to install it) as yet. Most staff accept disciplinary or institutional conventions on teaching and assessment without critical examination. They base their practice on their own experience, trial-and-error, or accidental knowledge of different teaching methods (Moses 1992a). For many this means the experience of how they were taught, not how they – successful learners – learnt best, enjoyed learning best, were challenged, interested, stimulated most.

In most countries it is possible to be appointed to academic positions without any experience of teaching in the tertiary sector. The formal qualifications are concerned only with the scientific credentials of academics or their equivalents, i.e. praxis experience or professional qualifications.

In Germany, but also in Australia, a lecture or seminar to future colleagues and/or selection committee or the university community is often the basis on which teaching skills are judged (Kalkum 1989). In some countries professors are appointed without interview, i.e. teaching ability is unchecked. In France there is a requirement of a certain skill, experience and expertise level for those wishing to supervise doctoral students. In Australia, too, the notion has been mooted that supervisors should be 'accredited' in graduate schools, should undergo some form of training (Moses 1992b). But this is for teaching at graduate level, and here the link is with research for which training is expected and provided.

Selection for the academic profession

The complexity of the academic profession is by no means matched by adequate preparation, and many institutions do not provide in-service training for staff to acquire requisite skills. This is true not only of non-tenured staff, already noted in Chapter 4, but also of permanent full-time staff. The academic role is also diffuse, because institutions, the academic profession and departments express different expectations. But, as Fulton (1993) has noted, these are semi-tacit expectations. Long-standing members of the profession or a department will know these because they derive from shared values, but those not socialised early into the discipline or academic work will find it difficult to sense them or to make sense of them. They affect selection procedures and criteria and the nature of staff development.

Department chairs recognise the importance of staff selection; indeed in a recent Australian study (Moses and Roe 1990), this was seen as a very important headship function by the highest proportion of heads. Yet there are not only departmental interests involved in selection of academic staff; institutional guidelines and expectations as well as governmental regulations may affect the recruitment process. Staff procedures and criteria may lag well behind the changing tasks of universities. In some countries, professors, for example, are chosen without interview and solely on their research records, as if the capacity to work with students, other clients and colleagues is unimportant.

In Australia, in the new system of higher education institutions within a Unified National System, a career structure has been agreed between the different academic unions and the employers (vice-chancellors) on a national level, which provides career progression from the lowest to the highest possible career grade, and which spells out the type of academic work one may expect at each level, i.e. specific functions, the general standard and the skill base.

In Annex 1 to this chapter is reproduced a version of this schema which shows the basic academic functions and the level at which they are to be performed.

The general conceptualisation of academic work has contributed to a hierarchy of esteem for different academic activities, with research highly valued and rewarded, and teaching and service seen as (un)necessary distractions from research, even in institution types which have explicit vocational orientation. Elitist values have tended to dominate the faculty conception of academic work (Boyer 1990, Moses 1991a). By contrast, the Australian conceptualisation (see Annex 2) envisages research, teaching and professional activities as being of equal value.

The recruitment process

Other factors than formal qualifications bear on the recruitment process and outcome. For recent graduates their pedigree, the prestige of their home university and their supervisor is paramount in the USA, primarily as an assurance of research potential. But social factors also influence the selection. In several of the OECD countries societal attitudes and government policies try to ensure that the composition of the academic staff body reflects various groupings in society. In the USA applicants from particular minority groups or women may be given special attention through affirmative action programmes or positive discrimination. In Australia equal opportunity frameworks at federal and state level prescribe procedures for enhancing employment opportunities of disadvantaged groups.

Legal frameworks in which the recruitment process takes place, and practices of recruitment, vary from country to country. The legal status of academics also affects the recruitment process; casual faculty appointments are more open to favouritism, are less likely to follow formal procedures. For tenured positions, particularly senior ones, the stakes are high and adherence to and avoidance of legal obligations becomes more difficult. Where academics are civil servants, different rules and rituals apply.

Anecdotal data as well as research studies agree on the importance of a research background for applicants, regardless what type of institution the applicant is applying to. Fulton commented (1993) that new recruits to the profession would normally have little published. Hence it is their academic pedigree, the status of their supervisor, examiners or department which vouches for their research potential.

While in the USA the prestige structure determines from which type of institution one is likely to recruit, and recruiting one's own students is avoided, in the UK Fulton noted and Eustace found, as did Halsey, 'incestuous' recruitment, presumably from departments' own PhD students, and within the prestige institutions. The use of external assessors or inter-university consultation is used as a guarantee of standards in the appointment of senior staff, although institutions nominated their own assessors. In Australia, too (Anderson 1993), incestuous appointment is common in the oldest and most research orientated universities, partly because they have had a monopoly as doctorate granting institutions until quite recently.

Staff development

Initial staff development

The need to keep active in research and high level professional practice has prompted provisions in most systems for faculty to take sabbaticals, research semesters, to engage in consultancies and professional practice concurrent with a faculty appointment. Generally, faculty are expected to advance their knowledge through continual engagement with non-trivial and practical problems. By contrast, preparation for the academic profession is one-sided, as we have seen, with preparation for the teaching function neglected. A wide variety of provisions can be found for those just entering teaching jobs.

In the Australian, German and UK systems, part-time teaching may precede formal appointment, usually as a job during research studies. In the United States, however, the graduate schools explicitly prepare future faculty by providing a broad education and in some cases (credit) courses in teaching, a practice advocated in Australia, too (Bourke 1991). Training teaching assistants has become a topic warranting its own books, even conferences in the USA (Nyquist, Abbott, Wulff and Sprague 1991); in Australia training of part-time tutors has been sporadic (Moses 1988), though development of resource materials for those teaching part-time is being funded by a government grant. In the former Eastern

European states, too, compulsory teacher education has been common.

In France, the idea of training for teaching/research staff is gradually gaining ground (Fave-Bonnet 1992). Teaching Centres for Initiation to Higher Education are the first training institutions for aspiring academics to be established in France, emphasising the teaching–research tasks of academics. As elsewhere, in France, too, for training to be successful teaching has to have a higher status.

If, as is the case, in many disciplines and in many higher education institution types a period of postdoctoral work is deemed necessary before an academic career can be entered, then clearly it is of benefit to create opportunities within and outside the higher education system to further develop both teaching and research skills during the period of postdoctoral work. The widespread use in the USA of teaching assistants particularly in research universities, in Germany of *Lehrbeauftragte*, in Sweden of adjunct professors, in Australia of practitioners does, however, beg the question whether research training is a necessary prerequisite for undergraduate teaching. In most systems the pragmatic answer has been no, even when uneasiness persists.

In Australia at least, a pragmatic response to recruitment problems has been to employ applicants who do not meet the traditional formal qualification requirements. It is then necessary to provide opportunities for gaining these during the employment. New academic labour markets are being explored: business executives, graduates not employed in the university sector, women, overseas faculty and professionals. These who return to higher education need opportunities for enhancing their scholarship and teaching skills through in-service education. More generally, new pressure for quality teaching, professional development and in-service training has emerged through external quality reviews.

In the UK, the Quality Council monitors mechanisms for assuring quality in teaching, which include a commitment to promotion on excellence in teaching, and the funding councils assess teaching. In Australia, promotion procedures are being rewritten to legitimate and value academic activities performed for much of their time by most faculty – teaching and service to the department, institution, profession or community in response to external pressures. The need for institutional commitment to the priority of teaching is expressed in the 1993 *Guidelines for Effective Teaching* (see Annex 2). A national Committee for Quality Assurance in Higher Education evaluates quality assurance mechanisms and monitors the outcomes. The impact on staff development will be considerable.

Disciplinary attitudes towards staff development

There are many barriers to academic staff development (Moses 1988). In the past such activities were poorly resourced, not institutionalised and marginalised. There was no tangible reward for acquiring teaching skills or general acceptance that one needed to acquire such skills except experientially. Staff development activities which addressed activities with a tangible outcome, e.g. writing grant applications, usually had good support.

The climate has changed. In most OECD countries governments are concerned about the standard of teaching, about the quality of graduates and of the standards of professional education. In some countries this concern is matched in funding for academic development projects. It may be expected that the disciplinary differences which have been observed in faculty's reponsiveness to staff development opportunities will disappear, once more funding is attached to it.

Generally, academic staff development opportunities are taken up initially by individual enthusiasts in any disciplines. But faculty in applied areas, in professional, particularly science-based, courses such as engineering and health sciences, find it easier to accept professional expertise in others and to complement their own professional expertise. Many from these faculties would have worked or have close links with external agencies and employers where employees make use of staff development opportunities. Ideally they are integrated into induction and career planning. These staff often are surprised when joining higher education institutions at the lack of systematic faculty development opportunities (Moses 1988). They are often utilitarian and instrumentalist in their approach and sometimes oblivious or adverse to attempts to change attitudes or values.

Staff in the basic sciences and the arts tend to be more suspicious of the discourse and the motivation underlying academic development, and to regard some of the offerings as 'technical'. Generally, these academics have less of an instrumental approach to academic development and if they participate seek to integrate what they learn through development activities into their value and knowledge system.

Staff development units

In Britain, award courses on higher education teaching and learning have been available for some time. Often, however, the participants are overseas academics. In Australia, graduate diplomas in tertiary education have been offered for more than a decade, mostly by distance education. Recently a number of universities have started offering graduate certificate courses mainly to their own faculty which integrate professional teaching practice with theory. So far none have made a formal teaching qualification compulsory. In Britain, too, institutions provide development opportunities for staff during their probationary period, and there is, as in the USA, a large variety of organisational structures.

The acknowledgment that teaching at tertiary level can be learnt and that faculties may need assistance has led since the 1950s and 1960s, and starting in the USA, to the establishment of a variety of services and units aimed to help faculty: instructional service unit, faculty development unit, advisory centre for university education, higher education research and advisory unit, centre for teaching and learning, *Hochschuldidaktisches Zentrum*.

These are most highly institutionalised in Australia and Canada with tenured academic staff in separate units. In Britain a national staff development unit supports local endeavours in voluntary training, and mandatory appraisal of academic staff is linked to development. In Germany, the Netherlands, and Sweden such centres have had mixed reactions from faculty and changing fortunes (Moses 1988).

Academic development units generally aim to assist faculty to develop their teaching skills, in equipping them with knowledge about and appropriate strategies to facilitate student learning, and evaluative skills. They provide opportunities for faculty to reflect and develop new skills at various stages in their career, particularly during the probationary period, in mid-career and in transition to other academic tasks. In most countries attendance at such courses is voluntary, sporadic and meets only short-term needs.

These units have been found more frequently in universities than in colleges or *Fachhochschulen*, possibly because college teaching loads were high and faculty's self-esteem was partially invested in their teaching ability so that no need for training by education experts was perceived.

'Training' in teaching, however, in any simple sense of the term, has not been found to be the answer to maintaining faculty motivation. There have been instead North American faculty renewal programmes, often generously sponsored by foundations. Alternative ways in which faculty can be remotivated may focus on career development and enrichment which may involve research and publication for job satisfaction.

Leadership and management

Leadership, management and service within the institution are, like teaching, mainly learnt on the job. However, over the past decade the 'middle management' role of heads of departments has been recognised and training is provided in leadership and management roles (Bennett 1983, Tucker 1984, *Higher Education Management* 1989, Middlehurst 1989, Moses and Roe 1990). Heads agree that they need courses in time, financial and stress management, in legal and industrial matters, in all matters concerning staff appraisal, motivation, and development. In Europe, the Conference of University Rectors (CRE) and IMHE provide brief workshops for recently appointed heads of institutions.

Leadership and management, as well as service, need to be expressed as legitimate roles of academics. Values and rewards systems need to change and acknowledge all academic and professional activities (Lynton and Elman 1987, Fave-Bonnet 1992).

Implications

At the beginning of this chapter we listed ten functions which higher education institutions must meet. Many faculty would feel responsible for seeing that their knowledge and skills were adequate to meet the demands of general, post-secondary education, research and scholarship and specialised education and training. Others would respond to the need for service to the community, acting as exemplars of national policies and performing leadership roles as they thought fit. But many would not realise the extent to which the concept 'general, post-secondary education' is being continually redefined; they would be ill-equipped to make the instructional and curriculum decisions necessary. Knowledge of educational technology, of other delivery systems, is generally minimal. Questions of efficiency and effectiveness, even goals concerning teaching, are rarely discussed. Thus any attempt to match the functions for which higher education is responsible with faculty commitment and acquisition of relevant competencies would show important gaps that need to be remedied.

This does not apply only to new and unaccustomed tasks. The core and traditional tasks, the pursuit of scholarship and research, are embedded and enabled in specific social and political contexts which have become more clamant. Knowledge of these, and skills in dealing with external agents – politicians, funding bodies and the media – are becoming as important for the continuation of research and scholarship as the research itself. Opportunities for gaining skills and knowledge in these areas have to be made available during the academic career, targeting those who provide research leadership and management, and educating the researchers themselves.

The commitment to access and equity by a number of member countries, too, pose challenges to academic staff not met before.

The implications for qualifications of faculty and staff development are as follows:

- Institutions need to develop integrated policies for selection and academic development as pre-service or in-service activities.

- These policies must accommodate faculty entering academe at different points of their career and with different preparation for it.

- Changing contexts of academic work require more flexibility, more concern with continuing professional development in all areas of academic work and the social and industrial contexts which impinge on them.

- Flexibility can be provided by removing some of the industrial straitjackets of university regulations which apply to all faculty. For development to be effective it must be responsive to individuals' needs as legitimised by institutional provisions. For each employed, aspiring or wooed academic staff member we need to consider:
  - what skills and knowledge does he or she have?

- which ones are needed to function at this level of appointment, in this discipline, at this institution type?
- how can he or she be assisted to acquire knowledge, skills and experiences needed?

- If access is widened to admit students who would have been called 'underprepared' in a more elite system of higher education, faculties must be assisted to meet them at the level they are at and to educate them to the accepted standard.

- If students with hearing and visual impairments are encouraged to enrol, faculties must be assisted in learning about strategies which make the learning experience for these students as successful as for other students.

- If ethnic minorities within the country are encouraged to participate more widely in higher education, and internationalisation is promoted, faculties must learn about teaching students who speak a different first language, about conventions of discourse and learning in other cultures, about different mind-sets and social behaviour inside and outside the classroom or laboratory.

- If women are encouraged to enter non-traditional fields of study, faculties must learn to evaluate their subjects and teaching to see whether they are gender inclusive.

- To encourage sufficient numbers to take up graduate study, undergraduate degrees need to provide opportunity for independent work, mentoring and peer teaching. Satisfying teaching experience during graduate studies could interest students in an academic career. During this stage, assistance needs to be provided for skills needed in order to be 'successful' academics, such as writing and obtaining external grants.

- Future staff for professional (applied) courses will be recruited from teaching and/or research positions. They will need leaves, secondments, and opportunities for professional and industry work.

- Some will be recruited from the professions on a full-time, fractional or sessional basis. They need induction courses to the culture of tertiary education to minimise culture shock. Staff recruited from the professions without higher degrees need support for research degree study or for otherwise obtaining research skills.

- Others will be recruited from a pool of graduates not currently in employment, notably women. They will need opportunities to obtain higher degrees, and/or professional experience, and teaching skills.

- Nationals of other countries will need induction into local culture, assistance with the local organisation of research, knowledge of teaching and students.

- Academic development is needed to assist all academic staff to carry out well their present work; to prepare for the demands of higher positions, and for shifts in emphasis between the different academic tasks. It should be directed towards sustaining motivation, vitality and productivity.

- In particular, staff are generally ill-equipped to make the instructional and curriculum decisions necessary to take on the full range of higher education tasks. Opportunities for gaining relevant skills and knowledge should be made available.

Annex 1: Career structure for Australian Unified National System

Academic staff are now employed at five career levels, A–E (previous nomenclature: tutor to professor; present nomenclature: assistant/associate lecturer to professor). These are the general standards:

> A Level A academic is expected to make contributions to the teaching effort of the institution, particularly at undergraduate and graduate diploma level and to carry out activities to develop his/her scholarly, research and/or professional expertise relevant to the profession or discipline.

It is clear that those who enter an academic career at this point are still regarded as developing in their academic expertise.

The general standards for Levels B to E academics add to or omit the characteristics and activities of Level A (deletions in square brackets, additions in bold):

> A Level B academic is expected to make contributions to the teaching effort of the institution, [particularly at undergraduate and graduate

diploma level] and to carry out activities to **maintain and** develop
his/her scholarly, research and/or professional expertise relevant to
the profession or discipline.

A Level C academic is expected to make **significant** contributions to
the teaching effort of [the institution,] **a department, school, faculty
or other organisational unit or an interdisciplinary area** [and to
carry out activities to maintain and develop his/her scholarly, research and/or professional expertise relevant to the profession or
discipline]. **An academic at this level is also expected to play a major
role in scholarship, research and/or professional activities.**

A Level D academic is expected to make **a significant** contribution[s]
**to all activities of the organisational unit or interdisciplinary area
and play a significant role within their profession or discipline.** [a
department, school, faculty or other organisational unit or an interdisciplinary area. An academic at this level is also expected to play
a major role in scholarship, research and/or professional activities.]
**Academics at this level may be appointed in recognition of distinc-
tion in their disciplinary area.**

A Level E academic is expected to [make a significant contribution
to all activities of the organisational unit or interdisciplinary area and
play a significant role within their profession or discipline. Academics at this level may be appointed in recognition of distinction in their
disciplinary area.] **exercise a special responsibility in providing
leadership and in fostering excellence in research, teaching, professional activities and policy development in the academic discipline within the department or other comparable organisational
unit, within the institution and within the community, both scholarly and general.**

We see that the general standards address teaching, research and professional activities at each level, increasing the responsibility, the scope
of the activity, and ending at level E with distinct leadership responsibilities for all academic activities.

The skill bases are also laid down:

Level A – normally:

> 4 year tertiary study and/or
>
> equivalent qualifications and/or
>
> professional experience

In many cases a position at this level will require an honours degree
or higher qualifications, an extended professional degree, or a three
year degree with a postgraduate diploma. In determining experience
relative to qualifications, regard is had to teaching experience, experience in research, experience outside tertiary education, creative
achievement, professional contributions and/or contributions to
technical achievement.

There is an acknowledgment that different disciplines or fields of studies, different institutional missions determine the appropriate level of skills.

The skills base increases over the levels; at Level C normally the following are required:

> a doctoral qualification or equivalent accreditation and standing ... and/or significant experience in the relevant discipline area ... a record of demonstrable scholarly and professional achievement in the relevant discipline area.

At Level E, the highest level, the skill base is as per C, but in addition

> academic excellence which may be evidenced by an outstanding contribution to teaching and/or research and/or the profession,

and recognition

> as a leading authority in the relevant discipline area.

Annex 2: Institutional valuing of teaching

From *Guidelines for Effective University Teaching*, Australian Vice-Chancellors' Committee, 1993.

Institutional ethos and climate influences the status of teaching within the institution and the quality of the students' learning environments. Institutional commitment to the priority of teaching would be shown by:

3.1 mission statements or aims which express the educational ethos of the institution and how it might be realised;

3.2 administrative practices, and practices associated with teaching-related services, which support the educational ethos of the institution;

3.3 adequate resources for effective teaching and learning, e.g. appropriately appointed classrooms, libraries, computer facilities, laboratories, and learning skills centres as well as support and technical staff, and the means of assuring that resources are applied effectively to achieve desired educational outcomes;

3.4 allocation of responsibilities which allows staff time to consult with individual students, and to conduct teaching as a scholarly activity instead of as a routine task;

3.5 a policy on academic appointments that encourages the recruitment of individuals with demonstrated teaching commitment, and on tenure and promotion which give teaching parity of esteem with research;

3.6 policies on matters affecting student learning opportunities, for example, policies on assessment and supervision of postgraduate students;

3.7 policies addressing ethical issues which might arise in the relationship between staff and students, for example, issues of abuse of power and rights to intellectual property;

3.8 professional experience or study leave programmes or provisions which allow for a focus on teaching, course design, teaching materials and curriculum development;

3.9 professional development programmes, personnel or units to assist all staff in defining and enhancing their teaching role and, in particular, programmes aimed at the induction of staff new to teaching, including formal courses leading to certification;

3.10 the availability of funds for exploring, developing and implementing new approaches to teaching aimed at improvement of student learning;

3.11 publications which describe and commend effective teaching and learning environments with the institution;

3.12 mechanisms for identifying and funding learning enhancement strategies, including English as a Second Language support, and literacy and numeracy support programmes;

3.13 procedures for the review of new and existing courses to ensure that programmes of study are coherent, properly organised, and that they provide students with learning experiences that meet the programme aims and that assess students in ways consistent with these aims;

3.14 procedures for regular contributions from students and external groups (e.g. employers and professional associations) into the development of teaching and learning practices and the design or review of courses;

3.15 a framework for enabling an institution to review and change institutional practices related to the quality of teaching and learning, and for managing change.

The AVCC recommends that each institution develop, within the framework set by these Guidelines, its own set of guidelines which reflect institutional ethos and priorities.

Chapter 6

Policies and Practices
The External Context.
Staffing and Demography

For the most part, this book has been concerned with the ways in which academic staff face new challenges and the effects upon their mandate, tasks, qualifications, conditions of work and staff development. We have sought to give a picture of a profession that is likely to remain committed to its own values at the same time as it responds to the changing values and needs of its social, economic and political environments. We now turn to two important elements of those outer environments, the demographic and economic frames within which academic staff must work.

Governments and university leaders should understand the critical importance of these external trends affecting staffing needs for higher education. Broad demographic developments in a country set the context, indicating the scope of likely demand for higher education as well as the likely availability of persons to perform teaching, research and other roles in higher education institutions. Economic trends add another critical dimension, sometimes by setting limits and often by presenting new expectations for higher education.

In the early 1980s several articles appeared in which the prospect of first an ageing and then a disappearing faculty in many of the OECD countries began to be canvassed (Fiebiger 1983, Wandel 1983, Bosworth 1984, Hansen 1984). A further concern, expressed in the policies of some governments, was that because higher education expansion had come to a halt in the 1970s, and because economic difficulties were in any case compelling reduced staffing levels, systems and institutions would not be able to replace those who retired by the same number of younger recruits.

This concern was by no means shared by all policy makers in all OECD countries (see, for example, Becher *et al.* 1993). In general governments and universities in most OECD countries pay only occasional attention, if any at all, to the impact of demographic and economic trends on staffing needs for higher education. While analysis is regularly conducted on their likely effects on enrolment, it is relatively rare that a parallel study is conducted of external trends affecting academic staffing.

From the middle of the 1980s studies were being set up which analysed the throughputs of staffing. In earlier studies adjustments to demographic and economic realities were not adequately reflected in the supply–demand analyses, which generally modelled the work done several decades earlier. The traditional conceptual model assumed, for example, the existence of a monolithic academic staff, with persons entering academic positions in junior positions and then devoting their entire professional working lives to academe. Most analyses assumed a largely stable student–staff ratio or, at best, considered limited change in that ratio. Many analyses made no separate calculations for different higher education sectors, despite clear indications that various sectors operated as distinctive labour markets, differing in their recruitment modes, hiring criteria and working conditions.

To some extent the later studies replaced the more simple 'melon going through the snake' (Davidson 1991) assumptions of a decade earlier by a complex picture. In this later scenario, multiple academic labour markets interacted with complex and multiple parallel and competing labour markets (Davidson 1991, Pearson and Pike 1989, Pearson *et al.* 1991, Sloan *et al.* 1990) so that it was implausible to assume that staffing stocks could be predicted on simple projections of recruitments at one point as retirements some decades later on. As we write, some countries (e.g. the UK) are beginning to work on the modelling of staffing flows as a guide to future policy, thus discarding at least some of the scepticism induced by earlier generations of manpower planning. Careful studies of the difficulties being experienced by institutions also began to appear (e.g. El-Khawas 1990). In attempts to increase the efficiency of staffing many systems began to consider changes in the working conditions (Konttinen and Välimaa 1993) and the rewards and incentives to be offered to academic staff (Pearson *et al.* 1990, Lonsdale 1993, Wilson 1993). We take up these themes later in this chapter.

Recent modelling of supply and demand

In Austria, Australia, Canada, Germany, the United Kingdom and the United States, special analyses were conducted between 1986 and 1990 to examine the nature and possible severity of a predicted shortage of academic staff (El-Khawas 1993). They apparently appeared because serious staffing problems were anticipated, especially in shortages of qualified persons to take academic staff positions.

Several of these studies experienced sceptical reception after they were completed. In Canada, for example, the Association of Universities and Colleges of Canada (AUCC) conducted a study of staffing needs for the 1990s; the advisory committee guiding the project called for re-examination of many aspects of the study and, eventually, sponsored release of a limited study. The Committee's members, which included experienced and well-regarded university presidents, continued to sense a discrepancy between the stark evidence of the demographic analysis, which projected staffing shortages in the near future, and the operating reality with which they were familiar, one in which considerable staffing flexibility existed and most departments were not voicing serious staffing concerns.

A comparable sequence of events occurred in the United States. Several detailed analyses, including Bowen and Schuster (1986), Bowen and Sosa (1989) and Atkinson (1990), were published and widely discussed. Each study projected staffing shortages and called for corrective steps to avoid severe problems later in the 1990s. Criticisms of these studies emerged, at first on limited methodological questions but eventually on broader grounds.

Considered at some distance, the problem was indeed due to a lack of fit. Both the studies and the reactions made sense but neither conveyed a full picture. The empirical analysis did not fit the operating perceptions and direct experience of large numbers of university administrators. There was a mismatch between the long-term perspective of traditional models of academic supply and demand, which were the basis of these studies, and the shorter-term operating realities of higher education institutions. It was not that demographic and economic factors did not matter. On the contrary, their central importance had led universities to make adjustments in staffing policies and practices throughout the past decade. In particular, as discussed in Chapter 4, many countries had introduced, or expanded, the use of academic staff in part-time or limited-term positions that provided a needed measure of staffing flexibility with which to meet changing student demand. In other countries, staffing needs were met by allowing the student–staff ratio to increase, often to a dramatic extent.

Another aspect of the mismatch between conceptual model and operating experience was that the hard realities facing higher education during the past decade, and likely to continue for the near future, were economic and financial, and these realities far outweighed any demographic changes affecting academic staff. With differences of timing and extent, most OECD countries have faced severe financial constraints with respect to higher education during the last decade and, consequently, have taken steps to reduce costs for higher education. At a time when enrolments have been expanding, the tactic has generally been to introduce greater 'efficiency' by reducing unit costs or, at least, by reducing the cost per student that is paid by the government.

The most telling evidence of this push for efficiency gains is shown in the changes that have taken place recently in student–staff ratios in several OECD countries.

As a comparison of the financing issues faced by various OECD countries (Williams 1991) has helped to clarify, fiscal austerity will be one of the most fundamental, lasting themes of the present era for higher education. Financial constraints, brought about by practical limits on what society can afford to spend on higher education, are a fundamental reality of mass higher education that has been only gradually recognised and is still not fully appreciated by many advocates of higher education.

Studies of staffing needs must be undertaken in full recognition of this harsh financial context. Continuing calls for greater operating efficiency can be expected. Increasingly, as seen in the recent experience of the United Kingdom and the United States, such demands will affect all types of institutions, reaching traditional universities along with newer, regional institutions and non-higher education sectors. Further pressure on student–staff ratios can be expected and will complicate analyses of staffing needs.

Continued reliance on a 'flexible' staffing component can also be expected; estimates of changes in the number of such staff will become a necessary element of staffing studies in the future. We have already expressed the need for sensitive treatment of such measures as the employment of part-time and temporary staff.

The next generation of staffing analyses will, then, be more dynamic than were traditional models. A differentiated academic workforce of permanent and temporary personnel will need to be incorporated into the analysis. Widely varying student–staff ratios might be considered. Economic factors will receive more systematic attention. Some parts of earlier models will be given closer attention, using more disaggregated analysis to inform specific policy issues. In using these data policy makers will not receive clear indications of what to do. Some data will be reasonably determinate, but others will be highly indeterminate, so that judgements will have to be made of what staff will be needed to meet which needs and against which supply possibilities.

Dynamic flows and models

Among the most important of the new elements of future models will be recognition of external competitive forces affecting academic staffing. Two separate forces must be considered:

- the prospect of an increasingly international labour market for academics, involving greater cross-national flows of highly trained individuals and, consequently, greater competition between countries – we return to this point later; and

- increased competition between academic institutions and other sectors, business and industry, government, and the nonprofit sector.

Both represent important factors that will affect the staffing picture for higher education in the future, particularly in the next century.

Data relevant to modelling

An urgent and immediate mandate for planning and governments is to develop improved information bases and analytical tools for monitoring these two external sources of competition. At present, information is limited on both international flows and on movements between academe and other sectors within a country. In the

United States, for example, a reliable time series of data has been collected for scientists and engineers, whether in academic or other employment, but not for other occupations and professions that have counterparts in academic positions. In many other OECD countries, comparable statistics are collected only for persons engaged in R&D (research and development) activities.

The OECD currently is sponsoring a project that will contribute to the needed cross-national information base. OECD's Scientific, Technological and Industrial Indicators Division has been working with UNESCO and with the European Community's EUROSTAT agency to encourage more consistent definitions and procedures across nations for the measurement of human resources in science and technology. At a workshop held in October 1992, experts and representatives from various OECD countries met to review the types of databases that currently exist and to discuss improvements in data collection. The workshop's agenda focused especially on a draft manual for expanded data collection on specialised scientific and technical personnel.

This current effort builds on other OECD efforts, including work that culminated in an October 1988 workshop and report, *Research Manpower: Managing Supply and Demand* (OECD 1989). The report reviewed available information from diverse sources and included recommendations for policy and practice. Notably, this report directed its advice to the national level, proposing ways that governments and national statistical agencies could include a wider framework of relevant employment sectors. Compared with the more recent 1992 workshop, however, the 1988 report gave little emphasis to the issue of tracking international flows of highly qualified personnel.

Wide adoption of a consistent set of definitions would greatly facilitate the task of monitoring movement between employment sectors and across countries. Progress will be slow, however, as member countries continue to have varying priorities and commitments to their own data definitions.

Competition with industry

Competition with industry and other employment sectors has become more difficult to face in the last decade, as financial stringencies and a lack of vacant academic positions have given universities less to offer in career prospects. Nationally regulated salaries in many subject areas are not on a par with those offered by industry and account for some outward mobility. Universities, however, can still attract and keep good people by offering more freedom than can industry to pursue scientific interests, to work with one's peers from other countries, and to secure rewards more satisfying than money. In some cases the best of both worlds is achieved when academic freedom is combined with the financial rewards of joint ventures between industry and university.

New approaches to age-related issues

The core element of supply–demand models of academic staffing has been the analysis of patterns of ageing among the academic workforce. Ageing patterns will continue to be central to such studies, but more narrowly focused analysis will emerge, as studies examine specific, policy-relevant issues. Such data must also be disaggregated by higher education sector or by field of specialisation, thereby allowing special factors to be taken into account. Professors in medical schools and in departments of chemistry, for example, have quite different career alternatives from professors of humanities or professors of political philosophy.

Also useful are studies that look to different age categories of academics. In Austria and Germany, analysis has focused especially on senior academics – those in categories C3 and C4 in Germany and those holding 'ordinarius' positions in Austria – because of concern that large numbers of incumbents in those positions will face mandatory retirement within the span of a single decade. In contrast, another age-group is of current policy interest in the Netherlands, the recently created category of 'research trainee'.

Another useful focus is to examine entrances into and exits from academic institutions at non-traditional times. The traditional model assumed that academic careers began for young persons with little or no other work experience, and then continued until retirement at age 65 (or later, in some OECD countries). This image may no longer be accurate. In England, for example, Fulton has recently reported that over half of academic staff at (the long-standing) universities have work experience in other employment settings (Fulton 1993).

In Canada, the AUCC study documented a significant '... flow of experienced academics out to other occupations ...' (Davidson 1991). Attrition among younger Canadian academics (ages 44 and below) accounted for more than one-third of attrition during 1984 to 1987 (Davidson 1991). This 'early-career' attrition has received little attention in past studies, yet other evidence suggests that it is sizeable and worthy of attention. A recent US study has examined the total amount of new academic appointments over the last decade as compared with the net increase in faculty that occurred during this time. Total hiring was about three times greater than the net increase, indicating that large numbers of persons take initial appointments but do not remain in academe (Carter and O'Brien 1993).

Studies of older academics – those over 50 – will still be warranted. As several national studies established, one impact of expanded enrolment several decades ago, with its concomitant additional hiring, is that a large proportion of current academic staff is now aged 50 and over (Fulton 1993). In the United States, they constitute about half of the professoriate, and in Australia 27 per cent of all academic staff and 50 per cent of associate and full professors (El-Khawas 1993). The overall profile of academics, then, is not that of even distribution across various points of the academic career.

It is just as important to consider subsets of older academics. The issues raised by having many who are very near to retirement are entirely different from the issues raised by a clustering of those academics in their early 50s who are still shaping and defining their scholarly contributions. The issues also vary by the special circumstances in each country. In the Netherlands, 'older' faculty include both full professors who are highly valued and productive in their scholarship as well as a contingent of associate professors who were judged to be redundant and down-graded during the retrenchment of the mid-1980s (Acherman 1993). In other countries, Italy for example, academics in their 50s would not be considered 'older', at least not in comparison with professors approaching 70 who are still active. In the United States, where retirement is no longer mandatory at any age, many universities are conducting studies focused on the prospect of having academics continue in their positions into their 70s.

Often, policy-relevant subsets will be defined according to both age category and academic discipline. Professors in business management might be older than 50 but still relatively new to academic positions because many have spent time in the business world. A predominantly older professoriate has different meaning in a field such as mathematics, where the most original work is done early in one's career, than in philosophy or other disciplines where senior members of the profession make the strongest contributions. The balance between older and younger academics matters more in rapidly changing disciplines – examples include high energy physics, information technology, cellular biology and literary criticism – than in more stable fields.

A second generation of staffing analysis

Based on these new factors and perspectives, the next generation of faculty supply-and-demand studies will be quite different from those that have been conducted in the past. Is it an impossible task? And will such second-generation studies be policy-relevant? Much depends on the development of a supportive 'infrastructure' of data collection, both within and across OECD and other countries. Several agencies – OECD, EUROSTAT, UNESCO among them – have activities already underway to develop the technical specifications for expanded studies of human resource needs that include persons in academic positions. National governments, in turn, must support the development of enhanced capability for monitoring the flow of highly qualified persons between academe and other employment sectors and, also, across national boundaries.

A recent study in Canada offers an excellent early example of the directions to be taken by 'second-generation' studies of staffing needs. The study, *Task Force on Faculty Renewal* (1992), prepared under the guidance of the Council of Ontario Universities and the Ontario Confederation of University Faculty Associations, involved a two-year iterative process of data collection, model building and debate focused on specific policy issues defined by Task Force members. Its work, which was disaggregated to five major disciplinary groups, covered many topics that had not appeared in most traditional supply–demand analyses. The Task Force reviewed a wide range of information, including: estimates of the current use of academic staff on limited-term contracts; exploration of the destinations of staff who left universities and the prior employers of new appointees; income data for doctorate holders in various employment sectors; and trends in doctorate production among Canadians studying in other countries. The Ontario study also developed simulations of academic replacement needs under varying conditions. This included allowance for political decisions (i.e. different funding decisions by the government), changing interprovince as well as international competition for academic staff, various adjustments in the use of limited-term academic staff, and changes in the number of doctoral students.

By taking this broader approach, the study was able to demonstrate that, despite some competitive advantages that Ontario universities currently hold, their future position '… will be largely dependent on external market forces' (Council of Ontario Universities and the Ontario Confederation of University Faculty Associations 1992). It gave specific detail on the impact of different levels of international competition and the vulnerability of higher education to competition from other sectors, especially in the fields of applied science and engineering. It stressed, too, that the universities are currently at a special disadvantage for junior, or entry-level, academic positions because of low compensation levels.

Recognising international cooperation and flows

For the most part, staffing problems have been seen as essentially the province of each individual country. Yet the international nature of staffing is beginning to emerge on the policy agenda. Whilst many maintain that higher education systems are as diverse as ever (Teichler 1990) there are also many indications of convergence. Although large differences in funding and payment systems remain, there is a general trend towards, for example, fixed-term contracts or greater distinction between teaching and research posts (Wilson 1993).

Whether or not systems are converging as a result of their own organic development, there are reasons to take action on issues which go across country boundaries. The issue has been canvassed for some time. Experts, sponsored by OECD and meeting in Stockholm, 1973, in a context of concerns about international 'brain drain,' developed an exemplary set of guidelines for surveying international migration of highly qualified manpower.

Some countries positively encourage internationalisation of staffing. This is inevitably emphasised more in the small than in the large countries (e.g. all of the Scandinavian countries and the Netherlands). Unions representing teaching and research staff are developing common policies and approaches and are considering areas of joint action. The recent EC Green Paper (1991) endorses the need to harmonise EC research staff conditions and career prospects.

In some countries already significant proportions of academic staff are recruited on the international labour market. In Australia, in 1981, more than a third of Arts faculty and faculty in the broad areas of science, engineering and architecture were recruited internationally. International recruits born in Asia, the USA and Canada increased from 1981 to 1986, while those born in the UK and Ireland decreased slightly (Baker, Robertson and Sloan 1993). As academics are seen to bring economic benefit to Australia, no labour market testing (i.e. no detrimental effect on employment opportunities for Australians) is required for senior academic staff on temporary entry or seeking permanent entry, while junior academic staff have to meet particular criteria. The vast majority of academic staff leaving Australia leave for employment in other countries, notably Asia, North America, the UK and Ireland (Baker *et al.* 1993).

International exchange is important for several reasons. The communities of knowledge are international and that fact constitutes an important element for the testing of knowledge and for the creation of excellence. Researchers have always found ways of participating in their international networks. Students, too, will live and work in an increasingly international world, and these needs require teachers to create new networks for exchanges and inter-institutional contact, and institutions to build up administrative capacities to service them. Small countries and those whose regimes have previously restricted the range of academic experience particularly need to have access to the wider human resources of the international academic labour market.

These opportunities and needs are being presented at a time when resources are tight and many other preoccupations are being visited on institutions. They form yet another set of issues competing for attention.

Central and Eastern Europe

Somewhat separate issues concern the staffing of Central and Eastern European universities. These institutions have received a plethora of visits, and with them a great deal of advice from Western European and American visitors. But structural and substantive issues of all kinds remain. The need to divest the academic system of remnants of previous totalitarian ideologies and practice are presumably well left to the competencies of the new generations of academics being recruited in those countries. Salaries are extraordinarily low and other conditions, equipment and accommodations are seriously inadequate. The re-emergence of these institutions into the European community comes at a bad time when it is thought that there are insufficient funds to maintain the Western European systems as they, too, meet new challenges.

There is already evidence that some of the Eastern and Central European universities are not able to recruit younger researchers because of opportunities to take up research fellowships in Western Europe and the USA. The general problem may become, in fact, that some of the most talented will naturally seek their way to places of opportunity outside their own systems. Greater interchange is essential. Management of growth may to some extent conflict with this desirable objective.

However, EC programmes have attempted to enhance mobility. The Tempus objectives are to promote the quality and to support the development and renewal of the higher education systems in the countries of Central and Eastern Europe. It encourages interaction and cooperation with partners in the EC through joint activities and relevant mobility. Several countries already fall under the Tempus scheme. Tempus forms part of the PHARE programme within which training has been identified as a prime area for cooperation. This is directed towards development of teaching capacities at higher education institutions as well as through staff and student exchange.

But there is known to be a problem in the brain drain of, for example, Russian scientists partly caused by the cutting of defence expenditure. There is also an internal brain drain where academics change their profession to get better paid jobs elsewhere. There is also a tendency to buy up manpower and technology on the part of foreign companies. Yet unemployment is also a major problem. Twenty to thirty per cent of academic scientists probably lost their jobs by the end of 1993. Somewhat different problems emerge in other countries, such as the defence of past privileges in Poland.

There remain critical success factors (van der Bunt-Kokhuis 1993) identified as availability of not only skilled manpower, of which there is much, but appropriately skilled manpower. Other problems are financial resources, infrastructures for communication and decision making, adequate managerial and linguistic skills, international cooperation and the mentality of people who have to be involved in the reforms.

Staffing of universities and graduate education

We discussed in Chapter 5 the content of graduate education as it affects the training of future recruits to academic posts. The extent to which the academic system can reproduce itself, and ensure that there are enough staff to continue the task of teaching and of providing and developing a knowledge base, rests partly on the extent and quality of graduate education for which, however, in many countries there are no explicit policies. For the most part, academic systems, and institutions, have assumed that there will be an adequate supply of graduate students of whom some of the ablest will seek academic appointments. In the UK, a recent policy statement (White Paper 1993) on research and graduate education in science and technology made no mention of the problem of graduate recruitment. One ministerial speech (Jackson 1990), however, offered the thought that all university teachers may not need to have doctorates.

Analyses of the flow into universities (e.g. Davidson 1991) draw attention to the uncompetitive position of universities in the labour market. The Canadian study concluded that to satisfy their own demand for PhD candidates, the university must expand their doctoral programmes and the number of PhD graduates at rates comparable to those of the 1980s. An Australian study (Sloan *et al.* 1990) showed even more serious shortfalls than the Canadian, although this was challenged by ministers (Baldwin 1991) on the grounds that the newly expanded and united university system may not have to recruit mainly from those with PhDs.

But the studies also show that the supply of those with advanced qualifications for the universities is highly subject - and time-specific. The market for research students, for example, in biochemistry fluctuates with the demand for the same people from the pharmaceutical and related industries. It is possible to distinguish between those subject areas which have a clear secondary market, and of these biochemistry, chemistry and, in other ways, economics are obvious examples, and those in which those graduating with doctorates have no preferred alternative to academic work. The field of history is an obvious example of this. In the UK, the great majority of those taking doctorates cannot secure academic employment and they must seek employment which they could just as well have approached directly after their first degrees (Becher *et al.* 1993).

Academic staff have uncertain destinations and the uncertainty begins from the time when academically motivated graduates decide to enter graduate courses. Government might find it difficult to usefully interpose itself in the academic labour market by controlling or encouraging the flow of candidates for doctoral courses and hence for academic work as it has recently determined to do in the UK (White Paper 1993). But funding decisions do rest with governments and it is certain that letting the market rule might mean that systems pile up shortages and surpluses which used to some extent to be anticipated.

The uncertainty will be all the more pronounced in view of the questions now being raised in some countries about the utility of the doctorate in higher education teaching. In a differentiated system, there will continue to be academically able undergraduates, the latter parts of whose courses should contain elements derived from current research. For them, too, the Humboldtian notion of apprenticeship may remain appropriate, although its application varies greatly between systems and institutions. For many others, however, as higher education moves from elite to mass and then to universal access, it is likely that their teachers will be better served by other forms of postgraduate education and staff development which will better equip them to meet the challenges of a wider range of undergraduate students.

It seems necessary for governments and institutions to make a thorough assessment of both the quantitative flows to graduate education and the kind of preparation offered within it. The analysis would have to be subject and level specific and also take account of the many different functions and levels of teaching that a graduate student might eventually be recruited, as a faculty member, to undertake. These, again, are issues that governments seem hardly as yet to have approached.

Academic productivity and the fit between supply and demand

Turning from questions of supply to the outcomes of academic activity, for the most part systems leaders assume that academics could be more productive. Many are tending to approach what they consider to be this problem through reward and punishment systems tied to outcome measures of performance.

Superficially, this seems to produce 'results', inasmuch as the number of students being taught and the amount of research being published has gone up in return for additional resources calculated at far lower unit costs. There have been studies (e.g. Kyvik 1993) which display large differences in scientific productivity among academic staff. In Norway, it has been shown that a relatively small proportion of researchers is responsible for the majority of publications: 10 per cent of the academic staff produce 50 per cent of the total output. The same study showed that whilst high IQ may be a prerequisite for becoming a scientist, differences in measured ability within this group do not determine subsequent levels of performance. There is also only a weak, if any, positive correlation between time spent on research and scholarly output. There is also a positive though relatively weak significant correlation between financial support and published output. The data show, however, a clear relationship between number of contacts and productivity in all fields of learning (this may be a proxy for availability of resources to travel and it may be that those who are most productive are likely to have most opportunity to travel).

Organisational variables do, however, affect research productivity. The average quality of staff at an institution has a positive effect on individuals. Frequent exchange of information among scientists working in research groups and departments stimulates productivity. In all, in fact, differences between departments of various sizes are not large.

If these studies suggest that demands for more staff productivity will get highly variable responses they also demonstrate that academic managers ought to work carefully with individuals to establish their working needs and the programmes that best suit them. Such procedures are perhaps all the more necessary for those who are producing less than they could. In any event the studies demonstrate that simply to rely on output analysis as a way of both indicating and stimulating success will be of little use. Outputs must be seen in relation to both the inputs and the processes.

These considerations affect the organisational framework for staffing policies in universities which has been discussed by Tavernier (1993). He advocates: flexible allocation of staff to allow for the development of excellence; development of a management strategy; the security of equilibrium through long-term financial monitoring; an analysis to identify opportunities and threats; a drastic shift to strategic management. Strategic management will use as instruments: recruitment procedures; criteria for selection and promotions; decision processes; delegation; reward structures; and staff allocation systems. There should be a broad recruitment reserve of young scientists on short contracts renewable on progress and with reduced teaching loads.

He argues for an end to departmental protectionism which causes vacancies to be filled in deference to demands for filling vacant posts instead of using allocations as a strategic instrument for the improvement of quality.

Implications

Many of the factors affecting faculty demography – the economy and the demands it creates on the system, for example – may be outside the control of policy makers. But certain ingredients of the mix are susceptible to policy action. They include:

- clarifying the extent to which numbers in graduate education will be sufficient to meet, within the very broad limits of plausible prediction, the needs of higher staffing; the nature of graduate education in terms of the changing tasks of higher education

- clarifying the extent to which institutions are resourced to meet the challenges presented by competing employment. Those problems that cannot be fully solved can at least be understood better if both national and cross-national studies, of age cohorts, disciplinary groups and minority groups are supported

- incorporating the need for international cooperation and transfer in modelling of staffing flows

- accepting that reliance on output measures as a way of increasing productivity will be of little use unless they are seen alongside the inputs and processes that enable good work to be done

- reconceptualising faculty as a national resource. Institutions could be regarded as knowledge and skill banks within which some, a core staff, will sustain the academic enterprise and offer continuity and leadership in research and teaching. They will attract many more able people who perhaps expect to stay for a limited period, but are available, without a sense of failure, to take up subsequent or parallel careers in the many occupations, public and private, that need personnel trained to engage in the full range of disciplined enquiry – from applied research in industry to public administration or consultancy. On these premises the system could think in more generous terms, in recruiting doctoral students and junior staff, than now happens at times when there are few faculty vacancies.

Chapter 7

Policies and Practices
Conditions of Service

In the past, academic staff have been thought well rewarded by their freedom and status, even if not as well remunerated as those of comparable ability in employment outside academia. They were thought well able to live with what they had. But everything that we have written so far indicates an uncertainty of task and mandate, and greatly increased pressure to meet a much wider range of obligations of productivity and accountability. These come at a time when institutions have no capacity to improve remuneration or other conditions of service. Given these circumstances, it is becoming necessary to ask why able people should want to come to work in higher education. For some, it is true, the opening up of the university to the ways of the market and of entrepreneurship provides new opportunities. But to many the main tasks are non-marketed work, and the discontents of most academics are a theme to which we return later.

Salaries, incentives, rewards

In many countries the incentives, salaries and other rewards open to faculty are rooted in the general arrangements for the public services. Two issues should be considered. The first is that of the problems associated with tenure; the second concerns the shift towards market forms of incentives.

The tie between academic work and tenure is predicated on the need for academic freedom and continuity of expertise, although it also derives in some countries from civil service statuses which entail something less than academic freedom. Tenure, however, brings with it relatively low salary rewards compared with comparable outside employment, although it also brings considerable freedom of operation in the use of time. The obverse side of tenure, as we have seen, is the wide chasm that has always existed between those who hold it and those who do not, and this problem has been accentuated in recent years. It has led to considerable inflexibility in higher education's staffing stock, not to be found in those civil services where transfer between jobs is possible. Attempts to loosen the tenure rules have been made in many countries and systems cannot avoid the issue if they are to make a determined onslaught on the cycle of opportunity and deprivation now existing in staffing structures.

Many systems are trying to complement and to some extent supplant the traditional academic model of rewards, with its tenures, academic titles and freedoms, by market inducements to those who perform well either academically or in line with other institutional objectives. In the past, only American universities have been able to offer widely differentiated rewards related to merit or scarce qualifications, although medical and law professors have received preferential treatment in other systems, too. Universities have not been able to hire staff easily in scarce subjects in competition with industry (see Fiebiger (1983) on Germany). In Australia, the decreases in relation to both other occupations and academic salaries in other countries have been considerable (Marginson 1991). But as salaries and career prospects have deteriorated relatively some systems have introduced differential payments (e.g. the UK, where the adoption of such a scheme was made a condition of government funding of salary increases, and Australia where market loadings are now negotiable). Institutions, too, have begun to consider their internal promotions and rewards and incentives schemes.

This might offset the trend noted in the UK for salaries for their most gifted employees to fail to keep up with comparable groups outside and for the range of salaries to narrow, except for institutional leaders and senior administrators where the distance from the professoriate has widened substantially. This is due to the bunching of academic staff at the top of salary scales and the failure to recruit many on the lower points, and to the fact that the lowest paid have tended to get salary increases proportionally higher than their seniors. In Australia, most academic staff are in junior or middle rank positions, with only 14.5 per cent of faculty above senior lecturer level (DEET 1992). A policy during the stagnant years of filling any vacant position at the junior level contributed to this.

At the same time, it is not clear that material conditions are the most important in finding and retaining good faculty. Job satisfaction, independence and the ability to use initiative have been shown in the UK to be more important than pay; those without academic tenure and those aged over 40 named job security as an important factor whilst those aged under 40 were more concerned with job satisfaction and challenge (Pearson *et al*. 1990).

Recent studies (e.g. Pearson *et al*. 1990, Lonsdale 1993), show that whilst there may be generalised dissatisfaction with the level of academic salaries, increased teaching loads and reduced research work are the most often reported effects of recruitment difficulties. The IMS survey of just under 3000 UK respondents showed that most attached considerable importance to a number of intrinsic features of working in a university such as 'job satisfaction', 'doing challenging work', 'having independence and freedom' and 'using your initiative'. A Dutch study (Timmerhuis and Vermeulen 1993) came to a similar conclusion, that it was the content of the work that kept them in higher education. In the UK study, some dissatisfaction was expressed in relation to career progression, pay and extent to which universities were felt to be democratic institutions.

In the USA, Canada, the UK and Australia appraisal schemes have been linked with individual rewards. This raises questions of whether appraisal can at the same time deliver staff development. Whilst in some institutions care is taken by heads of departments to separate appraisal for personal development from appraisal for managerial accountability, the division may be difficult to keep. It seems possible that some form of mentoring, of counsel by a senior colleague, separate from the head of department, would be more appropriate.

Problems are raised concerning the use of merit pay. There is, apparently (Lonsdale 1993), little evidence to support the proposition that financial rewards have positive motivational effects and lead to individual and hence institutional performance. There are also problems about the ability to measure merit or the lack of it. Lonsdale supports the finding by Pearson *et al*. (1990) that in an academic environment, intrinsic and socially derived satisfactions are more effective in raising the motivation and performance of the general body of academic staff than are extrinsic factors.

Job satisfaction

The evidence of the attraction and retention power of the academic profession is mixed. In the USA, a 1989 Carnegie Foundation survey of 5000 faculty revealed that 34 per cent were less enthusiastic about their work than when they began their careers; 20 per cent felt trapped in the profession and 15 per cent would not become college teachers if they had to do it again (Boyer 1989) – a small improvement in attitude over five years. In the UK, government data show that high quality applicants still seek the academic career and the proportion of candidates for research council scholarships with first class degrees remains (Jackson 1990). Also whilst in some subjects there are relatively high vacancy rates in the UK the average period of retention was in excess of ten years (Pearson *et al.* 1990); in spite of relatively poor rewards, academic staffing is relatively stable although there can be large changes in staffing levels in expanding subject areas such as computing or business studies (Pearson *et al.* 1990).

In Australia whilst there has been overwhelming dissatisfaction with the extrinsic aspects of their work – salaries, career structure and funding for research – 87 per cent of science academics surveyed did not regret their career choice and 60 per cent agreed or strongly agreed that their careers had been up to expectations (Anderson 1991). This may not hold for future generations. The proportion of honours graduates going on to full-time study in Australia fell from nearly 40 per cent in 1977 to 22 per cent in 1989 (Bourke 1991). In science, where students tend to proceed to higher degree study immediately following an honours degree, only 216 began honours courses in 1990, which will impact on PhD enrolment in following years (DEET 1992). In some subjects (e.g. biochemistry), recruitment to UK graduate work and, ultimately, the academic profession has been spasmodic, with studentships difficult to fill unless a particularly difficult employment season impels students to take them up (Becher *et al.* 1993). In Germany, too, in some disciplines fewer graduates than needed for reproduction of the discipline were taking up PhD studies, notably in the humanities and economics/commerce, but also in engineering (Holtkamp *et al.* 1986). In Australia, in order to make PhD study more attractive, the Australian Research Council has recommended that institutions define priority areas and that PhD students in these areas be given a higher than normal (ARC) scholarship.

The morale of academic staff is generally thought to be lower than in previous generations. Taken as a whole the pressures on them are greater although senior academics still enjoy a great deal of autonomy and in some disciplines those who attract grants and consultancy funds are able to buy themselves out of teaching and to set their own agendas. Dutch studies (Acherman 1993, Loeber 1991), however, relating changes in staffing structures and their associated conditions to faculty health and well-being, paint a more sombre picture. Those suffering most from drastic reductions in the number of senior positions available were those joining academia in the 1960s. They were now 'fifty or more years old and still assistant professors ... (and) ... feel trapped.' Loeber's study shows that both physical and psychological stress is consistently higher among assistant professors in the social sciences and the humanities: '... nobody cares for their research and teaching and ... given the chance to work in another department, their sense of well-being would have been far greater.' Figures in the sciences are consistently better. The general point is that academic staff may experience widely different opportunities which are as much the product of demographic chance as of personal qualities although these always play some part in determining career chances.

Impact on special groups

University decisions on academic staffing have been broadly affected by changes in the external environment over the last few decades. As already discussed at length, these changes have included a tightening financial climate and the pressures of accommodating larger student numbers and participation rates. Another environmental change that has affected staffing decisions is a general move, in all OECD countries, towards a social policy of encouraging greater participation of women and ethnic minorities in all arenas of life.

Universities in OECD countries have adopted policies and practices designed to increase the representation of women and ethnic minorities in academic positions. In some countries, governmental laws have mandated such efforts; in other countries, public opinion has been the basis for such change. The record of accomplishment is modest, however. In most OECD countries, women make up a small percentage of academic staff, usually less than 15 per cent for all positions. Only a few countries have seen the participation of women in academic positions rise to 25 or 30 per cent, reflecting quite recent gains. The experience of ethnic minorities is broadly similar: they are highly under-represented, although some progress has been made in the last decade or so. The particulars differ among OECD countries, with different historical events shaping the size, the relative status and needs of each country's racial or ethnic minorities. In the United States, which has had governmental legislation promoting equal employment opportunity for more than two decades, minorities held only 11 per cent of all academic positions in 1989.

The progress, for both women and minorities, is uneven across fields. In France, for example, women comprise 11 per cent of full professors, but with a range from 23 per cent of full professors in arts and letters to 8 per cent in health and medicine.

Universities and government ministries have developed a variety of strategies to overcome the barriers to the increased participation of women and minorities in academic positions. More strategies have focused on increasing the 'pipeline', that is, increasing the number of young people who complete the right curriculum in high school and college studies and who go on for advanced study. Support for completion of doctoral study has been a special focus, with some programmes offering loans and fellowships, and others also providing advice, mentoring, and research or training opportunities. Special recruitment strategies have been tried as well. In recent years, new attention has also been given to the informal socialisation processes that are part of academic culture, on the view that academe presents a non-supportive climate for women and minorities, often leading to high turnover and dropout or low productivity and failure to receive promotion. Mentoring programmes and other procedures to assist newly hired junior academics have been implemented in some settings.

The prospect is that slow progress will be made, even if existing programmes of assistance continue. Many of the general trends noted earlier in this volume will make it difficult for progress to be made. The structural changes and general circumstances of the academic profession are not currently favourable for any person wishing to enter academic life. Most of the growth in teaching positions in the last decade has been in non-permanent, junior and part-time appointments. Large numbers of young people are already in these junior positions, finding limited promotion opportunities in many countries or, in other countries, finding highly demanding requirements. The ranks of senior and mid-level academics have been reduced or, certainly, have not grown commensurate with other positions and with the growth in student numbers; at the same time, those who are in those positions are mostly at ages where they will continue to hold their positions for another decade.

These changes work to the special disadvantage of women and minorities, many of whom are in the midst of advanced academic study. And those women and members of ethnic groups who recently entered academe are disproportionately located in the junior positions that face limited prospects for promotion to the higher-status academic ranks. If anything, these circumstances suggest that tensions will increase over matters of affirmative action: expectations have been raised, yet actual opportunities have not expanded. Without new initiatives by universities and policy makers to reshape opportunities, the limited progress of the last decade may itself be threatened in some ways.

Unionisation

Higher education institutions are not perhaps the most fertile ground for union activity. The employees are individualistic. Many of them are both employees and part of academic management. To some, the residues of collegiality may make it difficult to think of the institution as the employer in the industrial sense. More qualified people want to become academics than there are jobs so unions represent sellers in a buyers' market. They hold very few sanctions, except those that would harm their students.

Where they have been effective, their successes seem to go against the grain of contemporary changes. At a time of greater and perhaps increasingly systematic differentiation of roles, statuses and remuneration, they seek more uniformity and equality of conditions and prospects. Where successful in tying salaries to public service salaries they have generally driven up costs. At the same time they have not been able to arrest the general deterioration and proletarianisation of academic conditions.

Yet the proposals in this chapter give unions an agenda on which to work, namely an insistence that institutions make an effective analysis of the academic task, that they work out optimum staffing structures and conditions in which work can best be completed.

Implications

In the past, it seemed appropriate to regard academic staff as individualistic workers who neither needed nor wanted their universities to do more than provide adequate conditions, remuneration and resources with which to exercise their freedom to attain excellence in their own ways. But leaving aside the particular problems of the academic under-classes discussed in Chapter 4, the position of tenured staff, including the most senior, is such that thoroughgoing policies and practices for ensuring higher morale and working efficiency are necessary. The conclusions that can be reached are as follows:

- The dissatisfaction, reported widely and in many countries, of academic staff with their roles, is a matter requiring attention by national authorities (on, for example, salaries and conditions of service) and by institutional authorities.

- Remuneration is an important factor in satisfaction and in many countries academics have fallen behind other comparable groups. But several studies show that more important are sufficient time and organisational space for work, and particularly research and scholarship, and the general regard in which academic work is held. Current policy pressures, from evaluation and quality innovations and to 'produce more', are also adding to distraction and dissatisfaction.

- In order to enable institutions and faculties to meet the new challenges, systematic staff development and career counselling is necessary. These would be based on an analysis of the workload and range and ways in which each individual could both meet the collective responsibilities and have space for individual academic activities.

- Whilst the recruitment of women to higher education has improved in many countries, they still achieve a lower proportion of established and senior academic posts. To some extent this is the result of the lower recruitment to undergraduate courses in previous generations, but is still a matter requiring attention.

Chapter 8

Policy Conclusions

We began this book by expressing discontent with the extent to which those responsible for the management and government of higher education were attending to serious gaps in policy and practice in academic staffing. Many of the problems may not be capable of easy remedy, but in this chapter we bring together the main points of concern which can at least be taken into account. We have summarised the whole book in the Executive Summary on pages 1 to 8.

Our points are directed to governments, institutions and to members of the academic profession. They need to be considered against a background of exceedingly complex changes in the purposes, functions and structures of higher education in many of the countries within the ambit of the OECD which we have analysed in this book.

Higher education is changing from a system in which much of the leadership has rested in the hands of senior academics, usually professors, working within small clusters of other academics. Permanent staff in most if not all systems were engaged in both research and teaching, without much differentiation of role, and institutions were able to work well without any very obvious and systematic management.

Mass higher education and many other pressures are changing that picture. Units and institutions have become larger. Research and teaching have both undergone changes in their content, client groups and organisation so that individuals often encounter a wide range of tasks. The new demands of numbers and kind have led to the employment of large numbers of part-time and temporary staff whose career patterns are both unsatisfactory to them and dysfunctional to the working of institutions. For all these reasons the changed mission of higher education calls for more sophisticated and careful management of human resources than used to be the case.

These changes should lead to new thinking about the governance and management of higher education. The new tasks call for new structures which take account of the proliferation and elaboration of roles. They call for more wide ranging and well planned forms of staff development. They should lead to the creation of structures which combine the vertical management and the horizontal collegial modes of governance and for the release of synergy between academic and management values. Roles should be specified to create the appropriate conditions for effective working together.

We are not able to pursue these larger structural issues in this account of emerging human resources policies. But in addressing our recommendations on our limited agenda to the different levels of higher education governance, we hope we will provoke thinking about them.

Role of government in stimulating changes

National policies

Some of the issues covered by this account are strongly conditioned by the policies of government and beyond the power of individual institutions to remedy. The first set of national tasks concerns substantive policies. The applicability of what is suggested below varies according to country:

- Many of the *rigidities in employment policies* derive from national, sometimes legal, stipulations. It is inconsistent for governments simultaneously to insist that universities should adopt market behaviour while keeping control over the numbers, levels and types of staff to be employed (Chapter 5).

- *Governments should therefore shed unnecessary regulations which hamper flexibility* such as the restriction in the number of hours to be taught by the different grades. These make it difficult for institutions to reshape their use of staff time to meeting changing needs, and convey the impression that professional standards are achieved if a certain amount of hours are completed. It should be for institutions and academic departments to decide how professional time should be spent (Chapter 5).

- *Agreement on institutional plans and negotiation over funds should provide a frame* within which national policies can be asserted whilst allowing universities the maximum possible freedom over the recruitment and deployment of their key resource.

- Difficult though it is, *attempts to anticipate staff shortages and surpluses must be made.* One remedy lies in *more systematic thought about the now considerable margin of temporary and/or part-time academics.* They are treated too differently from the tenured permanent staff, from whom they may differ only inasmuch as they were born two or three years too early or late. Their employment also creates hidden management and other costs (Chapter 4).

- Attempts should be made to accept a higher proportion of such people on *substantial full-time contracts which would vary in length according to the likely predicted demands to be made on the academic labour market* over the next decade. They would not be guaranteed tenure but would at least have the opportunity of full participation in the life of academia, and a reasonable run of time in which to build up their research and teaching competencies (Chapter 4).

- A more creative attitude is desirable towards the employment of part-timers and temporaries. Higher education institutions should be regarded as *human resource banks.* They will both provide research and teaching in the institutional setting and also provide recruits for advanced work in disciplined enquiry and the communication of knowledge in other public and private enterprises. There would be a core staff to provide continuity and stability. But many other gifted people should be able to come in as faculty for short or substantial full or part-time periods in the knowledge that they could transfer without any sense of failure to other occupations in which similar skills are valued (Chapters 4 and 6).

- Inter-institutional policies on a national scale are needed on the *content of graduate education as training and initial qualification* for academic staff and *subsequent staff development* (Chapter 5).

- For some future academics the present patterns of specialist first degrees and various forms of doctorates or their equivalent might remain largely appropriate. Preparation on planning and managing research, and on the systematics of teaching would, however, be desirable for all who are to become university teachers.

  For others, who will teach at less academic levels as higher education recruits a wider band of students, some *other forms of graduate education seem appropriate.* Systematic teaching in a broader span of content and methods than that provided by the doctorate, perhaps leading to a master's degree, might be more appropriate, although all experience shows that hard and fast boundaries in higher education do not work (Chapters 5 and 7).

- *Decision making about quality issues* has shifted from institutions and academic groups within them to quality assurance mechanisms prescribed or administered by the larger system. The emphasis of some national authorities on outputs at the expense of optimum processes is likely to do harm to both the well being and efficiency of faculty although expanded systems might make it necessary to have more systematic quality assurance (Chapter 2).

National data collection and analyses (Chapter 6)

Effective central policies should depend on *a comprehensive staffing needs analysis* based on both good data and on an eclectic values analysis. Some countries have been loath to build up any modelling or planning methodology which will enable them to be warned about impending problems. In some countries, research groups concerned with human resource studies have shown the way and to some extent filled this gap. But only government can launch a full needs analysis.

The contents of the analytic base would be:

- *A data base*. This would create a flow analysis segmented for different disciplines, for different career stages and different secondary markets over time. This would account for the changing characteristics of academic staffing, within disciplines, age groups, qualifications, types of institutions and countries and between countries. Both short and long term estimates are needed. It would be necessary to accept that many of the data would be indeterminate, and that only broad trends could be read from them.

- *A needs analysis*. This would attempt to state over time the needs for the different categories of staff in terms of likely trends in student demand, the needs for research in universities and in public and private sector organisations, the needs for consultancy, extramural teaching and the other identified functions of high education.

- A needs analysis would not be based exclusively on simple manpower planning. It should be based on consultation not only with the consumers of higher education but also with its providers and practitioners, and it should accept that higher education is not and should not be driven only by economic needs. A *multi-value analysis* would take account of the individual developmental and cultural objectives of higher education and not follow simply a narrowly instrumental agenda.

- Such macro-analyses would need to be paralleled by *micro-analyses of the nature of the academic task* (see pages 123–124). It is not possible to make aggregates of staffing needs without a more secure sense of what academics do and what is the balance between different tasks performed.

- *An evaluative frame* should be set up for each country which would enable assessment of the extent to which needs are being met on the broad and eclectic range suggested above. Present policies are not only intermittent, and in some cases casual, but are also implemented without evaluation of their ultimate impacts (Chapter 4).

Institutional level

Universities as well as national authorities need to clarify their policies and procedures. Their sense of mission must evince a conviction that they know where they are going and underpin their personnel policies. The future of a university is largely dependent on the staff it employs and good communication should enable them to understand and be committed to the institutional policies:

- *Institutions should devise explicit staffing policies. Their staffing plans should be linked to the whole institutional plan,* anticipating growth or recession in teaching and research and other functions, taking note of the age structure over the long term, and formulating plans within its financial frames (Chapter 3).

- Institutions should develop *integrated policies for selection and staff development* procedures which accommodate staff needs at different points of entry and throughout their careers (Chapter 5).

- Faculty must be assisted to work effectively with the whole range of students who are recruited for higher education (Chapter 5).

- Given the drive towards research which carries higher status and professional rewards, *decisions will have to be made about who does what*. The proliferation of work may also justify the employment of a more varied and flexibly managed faculty group (Chapter 3).

- It will be essential for institutions and departments to *clarify the ways in which resources, particularly staff time, will be allocated* between these tasks, and that individual members of staff are counselled on how to shoulder what may be more diversified patterns of work (Chapters 5 and 7).

- It is for institutions to work out ways in which *temporary and part-time staff can be better accommodated into an equitable and effective staffing structure* (Chapter 4).

- Women and minority groups are still under-represented as members of academic staff, particularly at the senior levels. Institutions should consider *active policies for removing impediments* to their equal advancement (Chapter 7).

The academics: faculties and departments

Academics, and particularly those in senior positions, are left with a considerable agenda of staffing issues. What we propose should be the responsibilities of those leading departments and faculties and the professional responsibility of all academics. It is a fiction that academics are strong individuals who can look after themselves. Senior academic attention to issues of task definition and staff development is required, and work on these issues in the departments should be endorsed by institutions.

We have proposed in Chapter 3 a new *academic mandate*. It would sustain traditional academic values so that the boundary continues to be drawn by the disinterested search for truth and respect for logic, evidence and demonstrability. It would also look towards the expression of more broadly based disciplined enquiry and to reformulations of the teaching task, to include the application of scholarly forms of discipline to the application and testing of research findings. It would also call for a reformulation of professionalism to include greater responsiveness to the needs and views of clients.

The implications of our book for the academic profession are as follows:

- It is a professional as well as a managerial function to consider the *changing range of tasks, to make priorities among* them, in the light of both personal motivation and the institutional and departmental portfolio and resources (Chapter 5 and 7).

- Senior academics should *analyse the conditions necessary to ensure that individual colleagues can meet their objectives and those of their colleague group* productively and with personal satisfaction. This should lead to agreement on individual development plans (Chapter 3).

Senior practitioners are naturally enough more concerned to advance research and teaching programmes. But the ablest set the patterns of work and role models for the rest. They may give a great deal of attention to the more promising of their staff, but not devote effort into thinking about the needs and potentials of all of their colleagues, including those not performing well.

- Those placed in leadership positions are not always well equipped to help their junior colleagues work out the best ways of achieving their personal objectives within the constraints of resources and the collective obligations. *Staff development for academic leaders is therefore essential* (Chapter 5).

- If they believe current *staff development programmes* are inadequate or inappropriate, it is for them to make sure they are improved. Engagement in staff development is a responsibility of senior academics and needs to be taken seriously. This entails working largely through the agency of *a properly resourced and professional staff development group*. Staff development *must be devised situationally*, that is, based on analysis of particular needs in particular places (Chapter 5).

- There has been insufficient *modelling of different academic work patterns* which would enable academic leaders and faculty to be more clear about what is required to establish the optimum conditions in which good work, along the whole range of tasks, might be achieved. We discuss this further below.

Modelling academic work

Present policies pay little attention to what factors make for good academic work. Hitherto, decisions on inputs have deferred to the professional judgements of the academics in the belief that they knew what was needed for good teaching and research. The new approach is to specify desired outcomes and reward those who achieve them and punish those who do not. This model has behavioural consequences. It creates a striving towards measurable outcomes but does not automatically provide thought about the optimum processes for achieving them or for attending to the second order issues such as the quality of working experience of either staff or students or other clients. Attention should be paid instead to identifying the conditions, the inputs and processes necessary to advance standards of work. In Chapter 7 we took note of the feelings of staff about deteriorating morale and conditions of work.

To model academic work effectively, so as to be able to specify adequate working conditions several patterns would need to be described, and different desiderata then negotiated:

- Work patterns would be differentiated to take account of the *discipline* within which the career is to be pursued. This affects the type of resource needed: equipment, technical staff, materials, time, and the way in which the working week and year are spent. Specificity is required; these considerations tend to be referred to in general terms such as the need for a well-founded laboratory or a well-stocked library. A laboratory-based academic must be sure of a firm resource base if experimental work is to proceed. Securing this often involves, as we have noted, writing grant applications, and careful management of the working environment. It usually involves spending a full working week at the work place. Teaching in these subjects also requires close supervision of students in laboratories or workshops. By contrast, academics in the humanities or social sciences require free time, often spent away from the distractions of the university base, and access to specialist libraries.

- The *range of tasks* that individual academics in different disciplines are expected to perform should be analysed, and time weightings noted for them. The stresses caused by the need to perform different tasks simultaneously should be recognised and priorities and selections made.

- The level and status of the institution to which an academic is recruited are probably the prime determinants of the faculty work pattern. Here the operational denominator is *the range of activity on the research–teaching scale*. This affects the balance of activities which the institution seeks to offer and its likelihood of attracting resources for that set of purposes.

Conclusions

We have outlined here gaps in both policy and practice, and in our knowledge of higher education staffing. Fortunately, in many countries groups in universities or in policy institutes or interest groups are building up excellent studies which illuminate both the substantive issues and point the way towards appropriate methodologies.

But knowledge about staffing is incomplete in several ways. Not all countries have acquired a competent empirical and analytic capacity for them to at least become aware of their own policy needs. In hardly any country is there connection between macro-studies and micro-analyses of academic working, including changes in the working patterns of knowledge creation and use. This kind of synoptic work is perhaps more a matter for creative policy analysis than research.

Finally, governments are still poor users of what knowledge already exists. It is high time they perceived this as the important policy area that it is.

Bibliography

Absalom, R. and Sutton, C. (1992) 'The Development of Effective Staffing Structures', *European Journal of Education*, 27, Nos 1/2.

Acherman, H.A. (1993) 'A Case Study about the Dutch Universities', *Higher Education Management*, 5, 3.

Åhgren-Lange, U. and Kogan, M. (1992) 'Strategies for University Planing: Meeting the Needs of a New Clientele', *Higher Education Management*, 4, 1.

Anderson, D. (1991) 'Recruitment and Career Development of Academic Scientists: Some Findings From a Survey'. In W. Cahill (ed) *Academic Careers*. University of Melbourne, CSHE.

Anderson, D. (1993) *Sources of Australian Academics' Qualifications*. DEET, Higher Education Division.

Arms, C.R. (1992) 'The Impact of Information Technology on Universities in the United States', *Higher Education Management*, 4, 3.

Atkinson, R.C. (1990) 'Supply and Demand for Scientists and Engineers: a National Crisis in the Making', *Science*, 248.

Australian Higher Education Council (1991) 'The Quality of Higher Education', Discussion Paper, NBEET, AGPS.

Australian Higher Education Council (1992) *Achieving Quality*. NEETS, AGPS.

Baker, M., Robertson, F. and Sloan, J. (1993) *The Role of Immigration in the Australian Higher Education Labour Market*. Australian Government Publishing Service.

Baldwin, P. (1991) 'The Government Response'. In W. Cahill (ed) *Academic Careers*. University of Melbourne, CSHE.

Becher, T. and Kogan, M. (1992) *Process and Structure in Higher Education* (second edition). London: Routledge.

Becher T., Henkel, M. and Kogan, M. (1993) *Graduate Education in Britain*. London: Jessica Kingsley Publishers.

Bennett, J.B. (1983) *Managing the Academic Department*. American Council on Education and Macmillan.

Bergquist, W.H. (1992) *The Four Cultures of the Academy*. Jossey-Bass.

Birnbaum, R. (1988) *How Colleges Work*. Jossey-Bass.

Bistrup, C., Keiding, J.T., and Tjell, J.C. 'To Facilitate Cooperation Between the Technical University of Denmark and Eastern European Universities', *Higher Education Management*, 5, 3.

Bledstein, B.J. (1976) *The Culture of Professionalism: The Middle Class and the Development of Higher Education in America*. Norton.

Blume, S. (1986) 'The Development and Current Dilemmas of Postgraduate Education', *European Journal of Education Research, Development and Policies*, 21, (3).

Bosworth, S. (1984) 'The Management of Staffing Reductions in a Time of Acute Financial Crisis: the Survival of a University', *International Journal of Institutional Management in Higher Education*, 8, 1.

Bouchet, R. (1993) 'Introduction to Teaching at University Level: A Special Graduate Assistant Programme', *Higher Education Management*, 5, 3.

Bourdieu, P. (1988) *Homo Academicus*. (Trans. P. Collier). Polity Press.

Bourke, P. (1991) Honours and Post-Graduate Students. In W. Cahill (ed) *Academic Careers*. University of Melbourne, CSHE.

Bowen, H.R. and Schuster, J.H. (1986) *American Professors: A Natural Resource Imperiled*. Oxford: Oxford University Press.

Bowen, W.G. and Sosa, J.A. (1989) *Prospects for Faculty in the Arts and Sciences*. Princeton University Press.

Boyer, E.L. (1989) *The Condition of the Professoriate, Attitudes and Trends*. Carnegie Foundation for the Advancement of Teaching.

Boyer, E.L. (1990) *Scholarship Reconsidered. Priorities of the Professoriate*. Carnegie Foundation for the Advancement of Teaching.

Boyer, E.L. (forthcoming) *International Survey of the Academic Profession*. Carnegie Foundation for the Advancement of Teaching.

Boys, C., Brennan, J., Henkel, M., Kirkland, J., Kogan, M., and Youll, P. (1988) *Higher Education and the Preparation for Work*. London: Jessica Kingsley Publishers.

Burke, D.L. (1988) *A New Academic Marketplace*. Greenwood.

Cahill, W. (1991) 'Tertiary Teaching Careers'. In W. Cahill, (ed) *Academic Careers*. University of Melbourne, CSHE.

Caplow, T. and McGee, R. (1965) *The Academic Marketplace* (second edition). Anchor.

Carnegie Foundation (March 1991) *International Survey of the Academic Profession*, 1991–93.

Carter, D. and O'Brien, E. (1993) Employment and Hiring Patterns for Faculty of Colour. *ACE Research Briefs, 4, No.6*. American Council on Education.

Castro, A. (1993) 'Building Bridges between University and Society'. In E. Frackmann and P. Maassen (eds) *Towards Excellence in European Higher Education in the Nineties*. Proceedings, 11th European AIR Forum EAIR.

Centre d'étude des revenus et des coûts (1992) *Les Enseignant-Chercheurs de l'Enseignement Supérieur: Revenus Professionnels et Conditions d'Activité*. No 105.

Cerych, L. and Sabatier P. (1984) *Great Expectation and Mixed Performance: The Implementation of Higher Education Forms in Europe*. Trentham Books.

CFAT Carnegie Foundation for the Advancement of Teaching (1989) *The Condition of the Professoriate: Attitudes and Trends*. 1989 CFAT.

Chronister, J., Baldwin, R.G. and Bailey, T. (1992) 'Full-time Non-tenure-track Faculty: Current Status, Conditions and Attitudes', *Review of Higher Education*, 15, No.4.

Clark, B.R. (1983) *The Higher Education System*. Berkeley: University of California Press.

Clark, B.R. (1987) *The Academic Profession*. Berkeley: University of California Press.

Clark, B.R. (1993) *The Research Foundations of Graduate Education*. Berkeley: University of California Press.

Cochrane, T., Ellis, H.D. and Johnston, S.L. (1993) *Computer Based Education in Australian Higher Education*. DEET, EIP, AGPS.

Council of Ontario Universities and the Ontario Confederation of University Faculty Associations (1992) *Task Force on Faculty Renewal*.

Davidson, R. (1991) *Averting Faculty Shortages. A Discussion Paper on the Canadian Academic Labour Market in the 1990s*. Association of Universities and Colleges of Canada.

DEET (1992) *Selected Higher Education Statistics*. Australian Government Publishing Service.

de Weert, E. (1992) *Responsiveness of Higher Education to Labour Market Demands*. Annual Conference of the Consortium of Higher Education Researchers, London Business School (mimeo).

Duhamel, C. (1993) 'Scientific Cooperation with Central and Eastern Europe: The Example of Romania', *Higher Education Management*, 5, 3.

Durry Report (1988) *The Condition of Teachers in Higher Education* (unpublished).

EC Green Paper (1991) *Commission of the European Communities Memorandum on Higher Education in the European Communities*, COM (91) 349 Final.

El-Khawas, E. (1990) *Campus Trends*. American Council on Education.

El-Khawas, E. (1991) *Campus Trends*. American Council on Education.

El-Khawas, E. (1992) '1992 Higher Education Panel Report, No. 82'. *Campus Trends*. American Council on Education.

El-Khawas, E. (1993) 'Demographic Factors in the Staffing of Higher Education: An International Perspective', *Higher Education Management*, 5, 2.

Elzinga, A. (1985) 'Research, Bureaucracy and the Drift of Epistemic Criteria'. In B. Wittrock, and A. Elzinga (eds) *The University Research System, The Public Policies or the Home of Scientists*. Almqvist and Wicksell International.

Enders, J. (1992) *The Academic Profession in Germany: Senior and Junior Staff in Higher Education*. Paper presented at World Congress of Comparative Education, Prague, July 1992.

Eustace, R. (1988) 'The Criteria of Staff Selection: do they exist?', *Studies in Higher Education*, 13, No.1.

Fave-Bonnet (1992) 'L'opinion des enseignants-checheurs sur leur profession', *Savoir, Education, Formation*, No.2, Sirey.

Fiebiger, N. (1983) 'Staff Policies', *International Journal of Institutional Management in Higher Education*, 7, 1.

Finkelstein, M.J. (1984) *The American Academic Profession*. Ohio State University Press.

Friedberg, E. and Musselin, C. (1987) 'The Academic Profession in France'. In B.R. Clark *The Academic Profession*. Berkeley: California Press.

Fulton, O. (1993) 'Paradox or Professional Closure? Criteria and Procedures for Recruitment to the Academic Profession'. *Higher Education Management*, 5, 2.

Gappa, J. (1984) Part-Time Faculty: Higher Education at a Crossroads, *ERIC-ASHE Higher Education Research Reports*, No. 3.

Geurts, P., Maassen, P. and van Vught, F. (1993) *The Dutch Professoriate: Myths and Realities*, unpublished manuscript.

Göbbels-Dreyling, B. (1993) 'Overcoming Staff Shortages and Blockages: Selected Experiences', *Higher Education Management*, 5, 3.

Gouldner, A.W. (1957) 'Cosmopolitans and Locals', *Administrative Science Quarterly*, 2.

Gumport, P. (1993) 'Graduate Education and Organized Research in the United States'. In B.R. Clark *The Research Foundations of Graduate Education*. Berkeley: University of California Press.

Halsey, A.H. (1992) *Decline of Donnish Dominion: The British Academic Professions in the Twentieth Century*. Oxford: Clarendon Press.

Halsey, A.H. and Trow, M. (1971) *The British Academics*. London: Faber and Faber.

Handal, G., Lauvas, P. and Lycke, K. (1990) 'The Concept of Rationality in Academic Science Teaching', *European Journal of Education*, 25, No.3.

Hansen, BL. (1984) 'The Impact of Faculty Age Maldistribution on Management in Ontario Universities', *International Journal of Institutional Management in Higher Education*, 8, 1.

Hecquet, I. (1993) 'Main Lines of Teaching Staff Policy in the Strategic Plan of the Catholic University of Louvain-Belgium', *Higher Education Management*, 5, 2.

Hengstler, D. and Lozier, G. (1990) *Projected Faculty Shortages in the United States: Implications for Europe*. Paper presented at the 12th International Forum of the European Association for International Research, Lyon 9–12 December 1990.

Higher Education Management (1989) 2.1 largely devoted to the training of heads of academic departments.

Holtermann, S. 'The University of Oslo Program for Central and Eastern Europe', *Higher Education Management*, 5, 3.

Holtkamp, R., Fischer-Bluhm, K. and Huber, L. (1986) *Junge Wissenschaftler an der Hochschule*. Campus Verlag.

Hommes, I. (1993) 'Active personnel policy to eradicate "grey mouse"', *Science Policy*, 14, No 4.

Houwers, J. (1993) 'International Exchange Programmes and their Effects on Institutional Planning and Management: the Administrative Perspective', *Higher Education Management*, 5, 3.

Jackson, R. (1990) *Academic Staffing – Problems and Prospects*. Speech to Royal Society, 17 July 1990.

Jarratt Report (1985) *Report of the Steering Committee for Efficiency Studies in Universities*. CVCP.

Jones, S. (forthcoming) In Brennan, J. Kogan, M. and Teichler, U. *Higher Education and Work*. London: Jessica Kingsley Publishers.

Kalkum, D. (1989) *Der Lehrkörper an Fachhochschulen*, Dr Phil. dissertation. Technische Universität Berlin.

Karpen, U. and Hanske, P. (1990) *Status und Besoldung von Hochschullehrern im internationalen Vergleich. Studie im Auftrag des Bundesminsters für Bildung und Wissenschaft*, 2 volumes. Hamburg.

Karpen, U. (1991) *Perspectives on Careers for Prospective Academic Staff*.

Karpen, U. (1993) 'Flexibility and Mobility of Academic Staff', *Higher Education Management*, 5, 2.

Katz, J. and Henry, M. (1988) *Turning Professors into Teachers*. American Council on Education and Macmillan.

King, K. (1990) 'Information Technologies in Support of Teaching and Learning', *Higher Education Management*, 2, 3.

Kivinen, O., Rinne, R. and Hypponen, K. (1992) 'New Clients for Higher Education and the Problem of the Closed University. The Finnish Experience', *Higher Education Management*, 4, 1.

Klasek, C. and Kuehl, R.D. (1993) 'US Higher Education in the Republic of Bulgaria', *Higher Education Management*, 5, 3.

Kogan, M. (1993) *Planning Faculty Staffing Needs*. Columbus Programme Seminar on Higher Education, University of Warwick, 23 February 1993 (mimeo).

Kogan, M. and Moses, I. (1992) *Staffing of Higher Education: An Overview of the Issues*. OECD Programme on Institutional Management in Higher Education, Thirty-Second Special Topic Workshop, Paris (mimeo).

Konttinen, R. and Välimaa, M. (1993) *Free Allocation of Teaching Resources as an Element of the Self-Regulation Strategy* (English Summary). Institute for Educational Research, Publication Series B 49, Jyväskylä, Finland.

Kyvik, S. (1993) 'Academic Staff and Scientific Production', *Higher Education Management*, 5, 2.

Lockwood, G. and Davies, J. (1985) *Universities: The Management Challenge*. Society for Research into Higher Education and NFER-Nelson.

Loeber, R. (1991) 'Situationele Doelgerichtheid en Gezondheidsproblematiek bij Ouder Wetenschappelijk Personeel aan de Universiteit van Amsterdam'. Thesis Vakgroep Arbeidsen Organisatiepsychologie, Faculty of Psychology, University of Amsterdam.

Lonsdale, A. (1993) 'A Changes in Incentives, Rewards and Sanctions', *Higher Education Management*, 5, 2.

Lynton, E.A. and Elman, S.E. (1987) *New Priorities for the University*. Jossey Bass.

Marginson, S. (1991) 'Will Academic Restructuring make a Difference'. In W. Cahill (ed) *Academic Careers*. University of Melbourne, CSHE.

McNair, G. (1990) 'The British Enterprise in Higher Education Initiative', *Higher Education Management*, 2, 1.

Metzger, W. (1987) 'The Academic Profession in the United States'. In B.R. Clark, *The Academic Profession*. Berkeley: University of California Press.

Middlehurst, R. (1989) 'Leadership Development in Universities, 1986–88' (mimeo). University of Surrey, Department of Educational Studies.

Mommsen, W.J. (1987) 'The Academic Profession in the Federal Republic of Germany'. In B.R. Clark *The Academic Profession*. Berkeley: University of California Press.

Moodie, G.C. and Eustace, R. (1974) *Power and Authority in British Universities*. London: Allen and Unwin.

Moses, I. (1985) 'High Quality Teaching in a University', *Studies in Higher Education*, 10, 3.

Moses, I. (1988) *Academic Evaluation and Development. A University Case Study*. St. Lucia, Queensland: University of Queensland Press.

Moses, I. (1991a) 'The Binary Experience – Success of Wasted Effort?', *Journal of Tertiary Education Administration*, 13 No 2.

Moses, I. (1991b) 'How are We Teaching?', invited paper for the Symposium on the Quality of Teaching in Higher Education Institutions, AVCC and the Senate Standing Committee for Employment, Education and Training, Canberra.

Moses, I. (1992a) 'Academic work reconsidered', *The Australian Universities' Review* 25, 2.

Moses, I. (ed) (1992b) *Research Training and Supervision*. AVCC and NBEET.

Moses, I. (1993a) 'The Development of Knowledge and Skills of Academic Staff', *Higher Education Management*, 5, 2.

Moses, I. (1993b) 'Against the Stream: Australia's Policy of Tertiary Integration'. In C. Gellert (ed) *Higher Education in Europe*. London: Jessica Kingsley Publishers.

Moses, I. (1993c) *Teaching and Research in Colleges and Universities. A Comparison between Australia and Germany*. Paper presented at the 7th ICHE Conference.

Moses, I. and Ramsden, P. (1991) 'Academics and Academic Work in Colleges of Advanced Education and Universities', paper given at conference, '25 Years after the Martin Report', University of New England, February 1991, and to appear in Meeke, L (ed.) *Australia's Binary Experiment in Higher Education University of New England*.

Moses, I. and Ramsden, P. (1992) 'Academic Values and Academic Practice in the New Universities', *Higher Education and Development*, 11, 2.

Moses, I. and Roe, E. (1990) *Heads and Chairs. Managing Academic Departments*. St. Lucia, Queensland: University of Queensland Press.

Neave, G. (1988) 'On the cultivation of Quality, Efficiency and Enterprise: An Overview of recent trends in Higher Education in Western Europe, 1986–1988', *European Journal of Education*, 23 (1–2).

Nyquist, J.D., Abbott, R.D., Wulff, D.H. and Sprague, J. (eds) (1991) *Preparing the Professoriate of Tomorrow to Teach*. Kendall/Hunt Publishing Company.

OECD (1987a) *Postgraduate Education in the 1980s*.

OECD (1987b) *Universities under Scrutiny*.

OECD (1989) *Research Manpower: Managing Supply and Demand*.

Parsons, T. and Platt, G.M. (1973) *The American University*. Harvard University Press.

Pearson, R. and Pike, G. (1989) The Graduate Labour Market in the 1990s, *IMS Report No.167*. IMS, University of Sussex.

Pearson, R., Buchan, J., Bevan, S., Jackson, C. and Stock, J. (1990) *The Recruitment and Retention of University Academic and Academic Related Staff*, Vol A, Pt 1, Summary, IMS Paper No.157a. IMS, University of Sussex.

Pearson, R., Seccombe, I., Pike, G., Holly, S. and Connor, H. (1991) *Doctoral Social Scientists and the Labour Market*, IMS Report No. 217. IMS, University of Sussex.

Perkin, H.J. (1969) *Key Profession: The History of the Association of University Teachers*. London: Routledge and Kegan Paul.

Perkin, H.J. (1987) 'The Academic Profession in the United Kingdom'. In B.R. Clark *The Academic Profession*. Berkeley: University of California Press.

Rajagopal, I. and Farr, W. (1992) 'Hidden Academics: The Part-Time Faculty in Canada', *Higher Education*, 24.

Rice, R.E. (1986) 'The Academic Profession in Transition: Towards a New Social Fiction', *Teaching Sociology*, 14.

Rice, R.E. (1990) 'Rethinking what it Means to be a Scholar', *Teaching Excellence*, POD, Winter-Spring 1990.

Schön, D.A. (1987) *Educating the Reflective Practitioner*. Jossey-Bass.

Scott, R. (1994) 'Campus Developments in Response to the Challenges of Internationalisation: the Case of Ramapo College of New Jersey', *Higher Education Management*, 6, 1.

Silver, H. and Brennan, J. (1988) *A Liberal Vocationalism*. London: Methuen.

Sloan, J., Baker, M., Blandy, R., Robertson, F. and Brummit, W. (1990) National Institute of Labour Studies, *Study of the Labour Market for Academics Report*, prepared by Department of Employment, Education and Training.

Smith, B.L.R. (ed) (1985) *The State of Graduate Education*. The Brookings Institution.

Staropoli A. (1986) 'Le Coimite National d'Evaluation. An Innovation in French Higher Education', *Journal of Institutional Management in Higher Education*, 10, No.2.

Statistisches Bundesamt (1982) quoted in Kalkum (1989).

Stern, M.R. (1992) 'The New Majority: Impact of Older Students upon the University Today', *Higher Education Management*, 4, 1.

Tavernier, K. (1993) 'An Organizational Framework for Staffing Policies in Universities', *Higher Education Management*, 5, 2.

Teichler, U. (1988) *Changing Patterns of the Higher Education System: The Experience of Three Decades*. London: Jessica Kingsley Publishers.

Teichler, U. (1990) *Changing Patterns of Higher Education Systems: Towards a Growing Variety or Similar Solutions in Europe?*. Paper to Conference of the Finnish Society of Education Science, 22–24 November 1990.

Teichler, U. (1993) *Quantity and Quality of Staff in Higher Education*. Paper to 7th International Conference of Higher Education, Stockholm and Turku, 13–15 August 1993.

Timmerhuis, V. and Vermeulen, H. (1993) *Arbeidsmobiliteit Van Wetenschappelijk Personeel*. Institute for Social Research Tilbury Ministry of Education and Research The Netherlands.

Trow, M. (1974) 'Problems in the Transition from Elite to Mass Higher Education'. *Policies for Higher Education*. OECD.

Trow, M. (1976) 'The American Academic Department as a Context for Learning', *Studies in Higher Education*, 2(2).

Trow, M. (1984) 'Leadership and Organisation'. In R. Premfors (ed) *Higher Education Organisation*. Almqvist and Wiksell.

Tucker, S. (1984) *Chairing the Academic Department*. American Council on Education and Macmillan.

van der Bunt-Kokhuis, S. (1993) 'Building International Networks and Alliances: New Directions in Higher Education Collaboration', *Higher Education Management*, 5, 2.

Wandel, C.F. (1983) 'The Challenge of Collective Ageing of University Staff', *International Journal of Institutional Management in Higher Education*, 7, 1.

White Paper (1993) *Realising Our Potential. A Strategy for Science, Engineering and Technology*, Office of Science and Technology. Comand 2250, HMSO.

Williams, G. (1991) *Financing Higher Education: Current Patterns*. OECD.

Wilson, T. (1993) 'The Influence of HE Funding Systems on Academic Payment Systems and the Supply of Academic Staff', *Higher Education Management*, 5, 2.

Subject Index

Author Index